PENGUIN BOOKS
Cromwell

David Horspool is the History Editor of the *Times Literary Supplement* and the author of *Why Alfred Burned the Cakes: A King and his Eleven-Hundred-Year Afterlife*, *The English Rebel: One Thousand Years of Troublemaking from the Normans to the Nineties* and *Richard III: A Ruler and his Reputation*. He co-edited *The People Speak: Voices that Changed Britain* with Anthony Arnove and Colin Firth.

GW00537981

DAVID HORSPOOL

Oliver Cromwell

England's Protector

PENGUIN BOOKS

PENGUIN BOOKS

UK | USA | Canada | Ireland | Australia
India | New Zealand | South Africa

Penguin Books is part of the Penguin Random House group of companies
whose addresses can be found at global.penguinrandomhouse.com

First published by Allen Lane 2017
First published in Penguin Books 2018
001

Copyright © David Horspool, 2017

The moral right of the author has been asserted

Set in 9.5/13.5 pt Sabon LT Std
Typeset by Jouve (UK), Milton Keynes
Printed and bound in Great Britain by Clays Ltd, Elcograf S.p.A

ISBN: 978-0-141-98869-6

www.greenpenguin.co.uk

Penguin Random House is committed to a
sustainable future for our business, our readers
and our planet. This book is made from Forest
Stewardship Council® certified paper.

Contents

For Jules

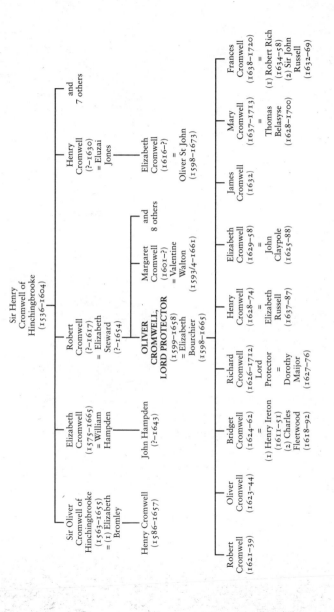

Oliver Cromwell

Introduction

Miles Sindercombe was a serial conspirator, would-be assassin and diehard revolutionary. The fact that almost nobody has heard of him today is because he failed in nearly every enterprise he undertook. Failure isn't always a bar to notoriety, however, as Guy Fawkes found out, and on 8 January 1657 Sindercombe's own gunpowder plot actually came a little closer to success than the one for which Fawkes had taken the rap, five decades before. Unlike Fawkes, Sindercombe at least managed to light his matches before his purpose was discovered. He had fought for Parliament in the Civil Wars, but had seen his cause and his commander's diverge sharply after victory was achieved. Now his old general was the nation's Lord Protector, who had shown no sympathy for the sort of radical ideas that Sindercombe and his fellows espoused. They were 'Levellers', dangerous opponents of the principles tying property to social hierarchy that most Parliamentarians had never abandoned. In the time-honoured tradition of extremists finding strange bedfellows, it was as agents of the exiled Stuart royal family that Sindercombe and his tiny band of two or three co-conspirators made their latest attempt on the life of Oliver Cromwell.

Previously, they had tried various ways to 'accomplish their devilish purpose', as the official account of the plot put it. There was a complicated-sounding scheme involving an 'engine' to blow up the Protector's coach as it passed through Hammersmith on the way to Hampton Court. A more straightforward approach was also tried: 'Once they thought to have done their work as his Highness was taking the air in Hyde-park; and, to make way for their escape, they had, in one place, filed off the hinges of the gates, and rode about with the train attending his Highness, with intent then to have given him a fatal charge, if he had chanced to have galloped out, at any distance from the company.' But his Highness hadn't, so on the night of 8 January, having bribed a guard, an old comrade, to gain access to the Protector's chapel at Whitehall, the conspirators 'went and placed materials for firing, which were discovered about nine o'clock that night; for in one of the seats was found upon the floor, a basket filled with a strange composition of combustible stuff, and two lighted matches, aptly placed, which matches had been rubbed with gunpowder, on purpose to keep them surely burning, and by the length of them, it was conceived that they would have given fire to the basket about one o' clock in the morning.' Whether this was really an attempt on Cromwell's life or just on his current home is not clear. Sindercombe may have merely been trying to demonstrate his bona fides to his Royalist paymasters. If so, they were not impressed. A Royalist agent reported that 'this powder plot required too much time, too many persons, and was subject to too many accidents, to be carried on with any reasonable hopes that it should succeed'.[1]

As with so many failed plots, there is something faintly ridiculous about Sindercombe's – though not about its denouement, as Sindercombe poisoned himself while awaiting his inevitable execution. But it is easy to dismiss the seriousness of plots when they haven't come off. The posthumous reinvention of Guy Fawkes himself as a ragdoll buffoon – despite the fact that his scheme involved enough explosive to obliterate the Palace of Westminster and all the people in it – is testimony to that. Understandably, the targets of such conspiracies take them more seriously, and Sindercombe's is no exception.

Sindercombe's attempted assassination emboldened those around Cromwell to try to settle once and for all the question that had hung over the government of England, Scotland and Ireland since the establishment of the Protectorate in December 1653. Sindercombe's plot had exposed the historical anomaly of the Lord Protector's role. Cromwell might well live in former royal palaces at Whitehall and Hampton Court; he might be referred to as 'His Highness'; he might have adopted much of the court ritual, both domestically and in his dealings with foreign powers, of the Stuart monarchy. But Oliver was not a king. Over the years, some of Cromwell's supporters convinced themselves that crowning him – something they had considered when he was first offered the Protectorate – was the solution to their problems. 'Such a settlement, as may secure him and us,' as an anonymous correspondent to a government publication put it, by which he meant, ultimately, making Oliver not one of us at all.[2] The 'Remonstrance' delivered in Parliament on 23 February 1657, a little over

5

six weeks after Sindercombe's deadly basket had been extinguished, proposed 'That there shall be a king, a house of lords, and a lower house.' The only way to stop Sindercombe and his ilk, it was emphasized, was to persuade Cromwell to assume the very office those conspirators' putative backers were trying to revive. Only then would 'the hopes of our enemies' plots be at an end'.[3]

We know that, after several months of vacillation, Cromwell eventually refused the offer. The question might then arise as to what he is doing in a series called Penguin Monarchs, even in square brackets. What follows is in part an answer to that question, and in part an extended attempt to ignore it. Some justification needs to be made for putting Cromwell in a list of kings and queens, particularly after he made such a meal of striking himself off it. Doing so may throw some light on the nature of kingship, the English and British interpretation of the role, and its historical development, which all seem like good things to attempt in a contribution to a history of the British monarchy. But Oliver is here, between Charles I and II, because to miss him out is to pretend that the decade between those two reigns is an empty one; or, at best, that it represents an attempt to govern Britain collectively, without a supreme head of state. The former ignores the fact that the 'Interregnum' is a period that encompasses, among other things, the first attempts at a real Union, the beginnings of the British Empire, and a bid to solve the question of a national religion in a radically new way – not to mention the readmission of the Jews, a people officially banned from Britain since their expulsion by Edward I in 1290. As for the second objection, the idea of attempted collective government, that might be applied to the three and a half years between the establishment of the Commonwealth in May 1649 and the beginning of the Protectorate at the end of 1653. But such a view also bears modification.

Oliver Cromwell, the man who dismissed both the parliamentary assemblies that sat during this period, and the army he commanded, wielded such influence that it would be another pretence to say that power really lay with the collective. So it would be absurd to exclude Cromwell from a comprehensive discussion of English and British monarchs on a technicality. Better to include him on one: a 'monarch' is not necessarily a king or queen, but a sole ruler. As Lord Protector, that is what Oliver Cromwell undoubtedly became. Miles Sindercombe certainly thought so, which is why he didn't wait for Cromwell to be formally offered the crown before trying his 'vigorous and bloody attempt upon his person'. Perhaps the real reason why Sindercombe is forgotten and Guy Fawkes remembered is that hindsight tells us the Protectorate was doomed anyway. But eight years after the last king had been removed, and six since that king's son had been comprehensively defeated and chased away, Oliver Cromwell's legacy looked to Sindercombe and his supporters, probably to the majority of his countrymen, at least as likely to last as that of the Stuart dynasty he had replaced.

I
Childhood and Youth

It is conventional to emphasize the obscurity of Oliver Cromwell's origins, certainly by comparison with the eminence he achieved. True, Cromwell's family was not just vastly less distinguished than the royalty he eventually supplanted (and, his enemies said, aped), but also less distinguished than those of many of the 'commoners' who have led the country in more democratic ages. None the less in Huntingdon, where Oliver was born in 1599, during the last years of Elizabeth I, the Cromwells were the leading family. In 1593 Oliver's father, Robert, had been the town's Member of Parliament, as Oliver himself would be – though it was as Member for Cambridge that he rose to national fame. The Cromwells derived their position from the head of the family, Oliver's eponymous uncle. Sir Oliver was a substantial landowner, who played host to the new King James I at his estate of Hinchingbrooke when James travelled south to receive the crown in 1603, and several times afterwards.

Cromwell's early biographers, permanently on the lookout for signs of future greatness, seized on the story of a childhood encounter between the young Oliver and the future Charles I, James's son, on one of these royal visits to

Hinchingbrooke. Naturally, the toddler-prince and his slightly older nemesis are meant to have fought at this play-date pregnant with historical significance, and Oliver is meant to have won. If the tale is too good to be true (which is no argument against its being true), then it is still a reminder that, as a guest in his uncle's house, the young Oliver is likely to have been in the presence of royalty. Despite the gulf in upbringing and expectation that separated Prince Charles and Oliver Cromwell, they did not occupy entirely different worlds. An observer at the time would have thought it unlikely, but not utterly inconceivable, that they might one day come to oppose each other as representatives of a divided nation. Englishmen had a long history of rising beyond their origins, as Cromwell's own ancestor, his great-great-great-uncle Thomas, demonstrated from a much humbler starting point to become Henry VIII's right-hand man. Oliver eventually outfaced his king with an insouciance that would have shocked most earlier generations, owing mostly to the transformative power of a parliamentary career and – surely even more importantly – a triumphant military one. But it was no miracle that he found himself in a position where his talents and luck allowed him to do so. And it can't have harmed Oliver's self-belief that Charles I was not some distant, godlike figurehead, but a flesh-and-blood contemporary whom he had seen when they were both children.

Only hindsight makes these reflected royal glories portentous. They were far from the main influence on the young Oliver's formative years. The first of those was, undoubtedly, his religion, and specifically the strain of pure Calvinism known to us, as well as to some contemporaries, as Puritanism, though Cromwell himself, and his fellow believers, tended to describe themselves as 'godly'. Puritans are hard to define because even at the time, the term covered a variety of different groups and beliefs. During the Civil War it began to be applied more indiscriminately, often simply to mean opponents of the king. For the time being, Puritans were still in the mainstream of the Protestant Church as settled under Elizabeth I. But they believed that the Reformation hadn't gone far enough in ridding the Church of Catholicism. They adhered to a strict interpretation of the doctrine of 'double predestination': that both the saved and the damned were already determined, and that God's grace could only be sought through faith, not good works. The practical implications of this were – perhaps paradoxically – not a withdrawal from the world, but a project to reshape it along godly lines. In worship, this meant an emphasis on Bible-reading rather than ritual, and sermonizing. Churches should be plain, unadorned with stained glass or images, and the communion table approachable by the congregation, not marked out as the territory of the priest. In Church government, episcopacy – the institution of bishops – was frowned on, though Presbyterians and those Puritans known as Independents, towards whom Cromwell would later lean, had differing views as to the suitable alternative. Most famously, Puritans had a (mainly deserved) reputation as spoilsports and vandals. They looked to a reformation in conduct outside church as well as inside, strictly observing

the Sabbath, and attempting to ban games-playing, dancing and drama, certainly on the Lord's day, and increasingly
at all. The destruction of 'papist' imagery and church furniture, including ancient crosses and interiors, was another
manifestation of this uncompromising zeal, with sporadic
surges of iconoclasm occurring throughout Cromwell's
life – though not, as popular legend would have it, usually
directed by him.

The lack of records of Oliver's early life and his family's
beliefs have made it difficult to assess the extent to which
this was the kind of religious grounding he received. Oliver
himself has been responsible for the impression that he was
a latecomer to the godly world. In October 1638, in one of
the most famous letters he ever wrote, he told his cousin
Elizabeth St John: 'You know what my manner of life hath
been. Oh, I had lived in and loved darkness, and hated the
light. I was a chief, the chief of sinners. This is true; I hated
godliness, yet God had mercy on me.'[1] We do not know
what Cromwell's sin was. Recently, it has been speculated
that this confession related to the murky story of a dispute
over his maternal uncle's land, during which Cromwell
apparently tried to have a sane man declared a lunatic so
that he could be appointed guardian of his estates.[2] This
seems plausible, and nothing in Cromwell's subsequent
career suggests that his honest and genuine commitment to
his faith stopped him from doing reprehensible things if
they seemed to his advantage – and then regretting them.
That may be why his legendary remark on the execution of
Charles I – 'cruel necessity' – rings so true.[3] But the likelihood that Cromwell repented of his conduct and tried to

live a more godly life at least by the late 1630s shouldn't blind us to the indications that he had been brought up in that faith.

Long before he wrote to Elizabeth St John, Cromwell's education had been on godly lines. In Huntingdon he attended the Free School, under the care of Thomas Beard, a clergyman and doctor of divinity – and author of a book with an almost parodically Cromwellian title, *The Theatre of God's Judgments*. Beard's own Puritan credentials have been questioned, and it is true that as an adult, Cromwell himself opposed his old teacher's appointment to a lectureship in favour of a more radical alternative candidate. But while Beard may not then have been a hot enough Puritan for the reformed, re-energized Cromwell, whether he was 'a rather complacent conformist' is also open to question.[4] Beard published a proof that the pope was Antichrist at a time when anti-Catholicism was briefly out of fashion (he did so anonymously, but a conformist would surely not have risked doing so at all). And his *Theatre*, with its memorable tales of God's interventions in human affairs 'against all sinners, great and small, specially against the most eminent persons in the world, whose exorbitant power had broke through the barres of Divine and Humane Law' (as the subtitle put it), certainly accords with Cromwell's later outlook as it emerges from his letters and speeches. In his very first recorded speech in the House of Commons in 1629, which if the speaker had not later risen to such great heights would be less than a footnote to the debate, Cromwell referred to Beard, holding him up as a positive example of someone who had risked a bishop's censure to give a sermon against another preacher's 'flat popery'. So while Beard's personal influence and own radicalism should not be exaggerated, the impression made by the religious education to which he introduced Oliver was surely deep enough. When, after Huntingdon, Cromwell chose a Cambridge college, he made a less than conformist selection: not Queens', where his father had been an undergraduate, but Sidney Sussex, known as a forcing-house for radical Puritanism. Cromwell may have strayed from the true path, as he admitted in 1638, but the lessons of Thomas Beard had clearly shown him what that path should be. Beard's former pupil possessed the zeal not of a convert but of a believer from his youth.

Cromwell did not stay at Sidney Sussex long. In 1617, just over a year after he had gone up to Cambridge, his father died. We know nothing of Oliver's relationship with his father Robert, and though he was Robert's chief beneficiary, he was not actually named in the will. Oliver was now the head of a household of eight women – his mother and seven unmarried sisters – more or less depending on him. While the Cromwells were well connected, they were not well off. Throughout Cromwell's life, until he reached the security of high office, there were times when he was hard up. Later, this could be ascribed to risky investments that depended more on religious faith than financial calculation. But his inheritance of a house and land in Huntingdon worth about £100 a year (around £9,500 today) was not much to keep a genteel household going. It was probably more because of his family connections than his prospects that in 1620 he managed to find a wife, Elizabeth Bourchier, who brought him a dowry of £1,500 and, in the course of thirty-eight years of apparently contented marriage, a total of nine children who survived to adulthood.

The 1628–9 parliament at which Cromwell offered his nugatory intervention quoting his old schoolmaster was made famous by a rather more significant battle, the passage of the Petition of Right, which tried to establish the principle that the king could not raise taxes without parliamentary consent. Though Charles I reluctantly acceded to the Petition, he found another way to circumvent it: dissolving Parliament, he did not summon it again in England for more than a decade. Cromwell, though, does not seem to have been involved in these tumultuous events. In the years before Parliament's return, and Oliver's return to Parliament, in 1640, the fortunes of a struggling fenland gentleman and a nation in the process of tearing itself apart on the questions of religion, taxation and the government of the three kingdoms of England, Scotland and Ireland could hardly have played out on more contrasting scales. During his early life, Oliver Cromwell took almost no part in 'great events'. If his early experiences were affected by national politics, it was probably no more so than for any comparable member of his class and religious outlook.

Historians of the period of Charles's Personal Rule – the years between 1629 and the reconvening of Parliament in 1640 – have recently begun to cast it in a more positive light.[5] For Oliver Cromwell, it was a time of trial, of loss of face and of position, which only began to improve by a stroke of good fortune in 1636. Although Charles I's increasing problems were partly of his own making, anyone in his position would have struggled in very trying political and religious circumstances; Cromwell, on the other hand, had no one but himself to blame for his local and personal difficulties – in so far, that is, as they can be reconstructed. Oliver's uncle had so badly mismanaged his great estate of Hinchingbrooke that he had been forced to give it up, selling it to Sidney Montagu, the Earl of Manchester's brother. Although this connection between the two families may have been the reason that it was under Montagu patronage that Cromwell made his first appearance in Parliament, the alliance did not last: Oliver got into a dispute with the Montagus over town politics in Huntingdon, which he comprehensively lost. The variance reached such a pitch, and the outcome excluded him so comprehensively from the corridors of local power – including the humiliation of being ordered to apologize publicly in Huntingdon by the Privy Council – that in 1631 he decided to sell up as well, and moved to St Ives, about five miles to the east. There, he seems to have slipped down the social scale. He was no longer a property owner, but a tenant farmer. He barely featured in the running of the town, and though his family grew (he also lost a son), his financial fortunes did not.

The Cromwells were well on the way to being extinguished as a force in local, let alone national politics. Perhaps this is why Oliver seems to have tried to have his maternal uncle Thomas Steward declared a lunatic, with a view to acquiring control of his estates. The attempt failed and, if it led to the bout of soul-searching that resulted in Cromwell's spiritual rebirth, it does not seem to have permanently soured his relations with the childless Steward. In 1636 Steward died, leaving his estate to his nephew. Soon afterwards, Cromwell and his family moved to Ely, taking up residence in a house (which still stands) near St Mary's Church. Steward's estate included land and property in Ely and nearby villages, and made the thirty-seven-year-old Cromwell financially secure for the first time since reaching adulthood.

He also returned to a more prominent role in local politics. As he had already shown, Cromwell had something of a flair for controversy. To his disputes in Huntingdon and over Steward's lands can be added his part in supporting opponents of the fen drainage scheme in his locality, which threatened to enclose common land and pass it into private hands. '[A] crowd of women and men, armed with scythes and pitchforks, uttered threatening words against any one that should drive their fens. It was commonly reported by the commoners in Ely Fens, and the fens adjoining, that Mr Cromwell, of Ely, had undertaken, they paying him a groat [4d, worth perhaps £1.50 today] for every cow they had upon the common, to hold the drainers in suit of law for five years, and that in the meantime they should enjoy every foot of their common.'[6] It may be tempting to see here the first stirrings of Cromwell the organizer and leader of men, and Royalist propagandists later made sneering references to him as 'Lord of the Fens', but, as with so much of his early life (and a significant portion even of his later life), we cannot know what motivated

Cromwell, or how he viewed this struggle. None the less, as the drainage scheme had recently come under royal control, Cromwell's stand, such as it was, added to the growing opposition to Charles I on several more urgent fronts.

The Personal Rule came to an end in April 1640. The king's failed attempt to impose a prayer book based on the English Book of Common Prayer and strengthened episcopal government on Scottish Presbyterians had eventually led to armed confrontation with representatives of the Scots' Solemn League and Covenant. The Covenanters, taking an oath only to obey a king who supported a Presbyterian Church, humiliated an English army at Kelso, which took flight without engaging. To resume the so-called Bishops' Wars, Charles needed money, and only a recalled Westminster Parliament could grant him sufficient funds. Faced with an open armed rebellion in one of his kingdoms, the king thought he had a right to expect his English MPs to provide him with the means to resist it. Many of those MPs, however, had other matters on their minds, were in any case sympathetic to the Covenanters' cause, and saw Charles's difficulties as an opportunity to raise their own issues. Years of questionable royal financial demands and objectionable religious innovations had given rise to an even more coherent opposition in England than had first moved Charles to dispense with Parliament. The strongest element of this opposition was to be found among the Puritan gentry. A new addition to their ranks, sitting for the first time as one of two Members for Cambridge, was Oliver Cromwell.

2

At Westminster

In just over two years, between April 1640 and August 1642, the growing parliamentary opposition to the king brought England and Wales to civil war. (Of Charles's three kingdoms, two – Scotland and Ireland – actually took up arms before 1642.) The new Member for Cambridge in the Short Parliament that sat for less than a month, and who retained his seat in the Long Parliament that was summoned in November 1640 and sat for more than a decade, was emphatically not a major player in this descent to all-out conflict. Our knowledge of where Oliver Cromwell ended up can make it difficult to accept that he was in fact a relatively obscure figure well into the Civil War. Cromwell might never have become a military leader if he had not first been an MP. But it was as a soldier, not a politician, that he made his name, establishing himself in the national consciousness in spite of, not because of, his position in Parliament.

But Cromwell did not spring from complete anonymity. His own family connections included men who were at the centre of the controversies of the day. One of the most keenly contested issues that had arisen during Charles's Personal Rule was the dispute over ship money, an extra-parliamentary levy raised by his government in order to pay for naval costs, but one now enforced throughout the country, beyond the coastal counties to which it had previously been confined. By 1636, ship money had become a much-resented annual levy, and in 1637 Charles had decided to prosecute one of the most prominent refuseniks: a Buckinghamshire MP called John Hampden, who a decade previously had also refused to pay the king's forced loan. Hampden was from a gentry family of no great wealth or influence, but he had allied himself to the Puritan opposition in the Commons and its supporters in the Lords, including John Pym (the Hampshire MP who through the 1620s and 1630s emerged as the leading voice of Puritanism in the Commons) and Viscount Saye and Sele (a powerful, godly influence in the Lords). Hampden's mother was Elizabeth Cromwell, paternal aunt to Oliver, so Hampden and Cromwell were first cousins. Hampden's legal counsel in the ship money case was Oliver St John, who would shortly marry another Cromwell cousin, the Elizabeth to whom Cromwell wrote of his spiritual rebirth in 1638. As far as our understanding of Cromwell is concerned, the outcome of the case (Hampden lost, but narrowly and technically enough to give encouragement to supporters of his stand) was less important than the circles to which it relates him. Cromwell's extended godly family were leading figures in the opposition to Charles I.

For Cromwell and his fellow Puritans, as for the Scots Covenanters, opposition to the king centred on matters of religion. This was true of Cromwell from the very beginning of his parliamentary career. It is arguable that, for all the momentous issues that concentrated his mind for the rest of his life, religion remained his principal concern. In this he was not, in the seventeenth century, unique, or even unusual. Cromwell himself, like many of his contemporaries, would have in any case found the distinction between religious and political concerns a false one. For them, religion was not a part of life, but the point of it. Political questions were seen and debated through the prism of Providence, and the chief guide to political conduct was discerning the mind of God. What can seem at this distance in time to be a squabble over the technical niceties of Protestant ritual was given urgency in Cromwell's time by the genuine fear of Catholicism – 'popery'. It is with this in mind that we should view the reaction to Charles's promotion in 1633 of William Laud to the head of the Church of England as Archbishop of Canterbury.

Laud was a churchman so far removed from Puritanism that he had twice been offered a cardinal's hat (though he had refused). An enthusiastic embracer and enforcer of conformity in the Church, he emphasized the importance of the altar rather than the pulpit; the Prayer Book; and ceremonial in general, in a way that his opponents alleged made him an 'Arminian', a follower of the Dutch theologian of that name whose teachings on predestination Puritans saw as little better than 'popery'. To the godly, such as Cromwell and his new allies, Laud's position and his conduct in it were a provocation. Like his opponents, Laud saw the political and the religious as intrinsically connected, telling the king that 'if it [the Church] had more

21

power, the Kinge might have more both obedience and service'.[1]

In the first days of the spring 1640 Parliament, various godly MPs, including John Pym, raised their objections to Charles's conduct of government, and made it clear that only after these were resolved would they move to supplying the king with finance for his war. When Charles realized that he was not likely to get any money out of Parliament, he swiftly dissolved it, after only three weeks, on 5 May. This arbitrary decision inflamed opinion beyond Westminster and, significantly, when crowds took to the streets in London after the dissolution, it was on Archbishop Laud that they turned their anger. There were threats to burn down Lambeth Palace, and Laud himself was forced to flee. The first indications in England that opposition to the king had moved well beyond a small group of disaffected 'hot' Protestant gentry were beginning to emerge. Here was a new element in English politics. In earlier periods, popular uprising had been sporadic, and had tended to unite establishment resistance to it. From the 1640s, those inside Parliament were forced to bear in mind the tide of popular opinion – especially as it would increasingly be revealed in the circulation of political pamphlets – and often to follow it. Later, this radical popular element would be institutionalized in the New Model Army, which for a decade became a leading player in domestic politics, and as he rose to prominence, Cromwell himself learned how to appeal to or circumvent the popular will. Cromwell's own interventions during his early parliamentary career were not momentous, though they weren't negligible. But the experience, not only of sitting in Parliament as great events unfolded, but also of witnessing the tumult generated in the London streets, was a political education that he would not forget. Cromwell's early parliamentary career is significant not only for what Cromwell did in Parliament, but for what Parliament – and the city it stood in – did to Cromwell.

He only had to wait six months before resuming his apprenticeship. Charles's attempt to re-engage the Scots Covenanters ended in disaster, when the rebels crossed into England and defeated a Royalist army at Newburn, outside Newcastle, on 29 August 1640, occupying Newcastle itself. By this time, several English peers had begun to co-ordinate with the Covenanters to bring pressure on the king to negotiate. Twelve lords, including future leaders of Parliament's armies such as the Earls of Essex and Warwick, had petitioned him to recall Parliament. There is evidence, too, of a substantial English Puritan effort to raise money for the Scots.[2] When Charles did re-summon Parliament for November 1640, it was not to raise money for war, but to pay for a peace treaty. The terms of the Treaty of Ripon were a humiliation for Charles, but not for many English subjects who had more or less tacitly supported the Covenanters' cause. Still, the English taxpayer had to finance the Scottish victors: it was agreed that the Covenanters would remain in the six northern counties of England for the time being, and would be paid £850 a day while they did so.

Most accounts of the months during which the Long

Parliament's confrontation with Charles and his allies split the country barely mention Oliver Cromwell. In the great matters that preoccupied the House and the king – the impeachment of Charles's chief minister, Thomas Went-worth, Earl of Strafford, on grounds of treason and tyranny for his actions on behalf of the king in Ireland and against the Scots Covenanters, the debate on the Grand Remon-strance, which set out a catalogue of the king's errors and abuses from his accession to the present, even the Root and Branch debate, which considered the possibility of abolishing the office of bishops in the Church of England – Cromwell played a minor role at most. He was capable of a neophyte's confident misreading of the runes, as when he assured the Royalist Lord Falkland that the Remonstrance was so well supported that it didn't even need to be debated. In fact, the debate lasted for sixteen hours, and – as Falk-land reminded Cromwell afterwards – passed by a mere eleven votes. This was clear evidence that, for all the energy of the parliamentary opposition to Charles, it was far from united, not only because confronting their sovereign was still a step too far for some, but also because those who might oppose Charles did not necessarily agree on other fundamentals, such as religious policy. Even after the split between Parliamentarians and Royalists, the strains of keeping a united front were acutely felt on Parliament's side, where opposition to the king had created unnatural alliances, of Presbyterians and Independents, of social reformers and titled landowners. None the less, his time in Parliament saw Cromwell emerge as a vigorous and active if junior member of a group of like-minded MPs who were driving the parliamentary agenda. Appearing on committees, managing petitions, liaising between the Commons and the Lords, Cromwell placed himself in the midst of what became known as the 'Junto', under the (informal) leadership of John Pym in the Commons and the Earl of Bedford in the Lords. As the Parliament proceeded, Cromwell made a small impression as a presenter of petitions on behalf of other Puritans who had fallen foul of Charles's administration, including the future anti-hierarchical 'Leveller', John Lilburne. Lilburne was set free four days later, the beginning of a complicated relationship between two men of unshakeable will who were not always on the same side.

Descriptions of Cromwell at this time were mostly written in hindsight, once he had achieved his fame. One of the best known is that of Edward Hyde, future Royalist Earl of Clarendon and historian of the 'Rebellion', who was confronted by Cromwell in a committee that Hyde was chairing. 'Cromwell (who had never before been heard to speak in the house of commons) ordered the witnesses and petitioners in the manner of proceeding ... [He] in great fury reproached the chairman for being partial, and that he discountenanced the witnesses by threatening them: the other [i.e. Hyde] appealed to the committee, which justified him, and declared that he behaved himself as he ought to do; which more inflamed him, who was already too much angry ... In the end, his whole carriage was so tempestuous, and his behaviour so insolent, that the chairman found himself obliged to reprehend him.' For that, Clarendon writes, 'he never forgave; and took all occasions afterwards to pursue him with the utmost malice and revenge, to his death'.[3] At the time, Clarendon was in fact no more experienced as an MP than Cromwell – who had, of course, 'been heard to speak' already on numerous occasions – as well as being ten years his junior. The impression of patrician savoir-faire given in Clarendon's memoirs can be as misleading about his own status as that of his adversary. To set against the partial memoirs of an inveterate enemy, there is John Hampden's approving comment made at the time of Oliver's early parliamentary career that Cromwell was 'one that would sit well at the mark'.[4] While it isn't exactly clear what Hampden meant by this – was Cromwell prepared to take matters to the limit? was he focused on his goal? – its positive tone was definitely not influenced by Cromwell's subsequent rise, as Hampden died in 1643.

Somewhere between these two accounts lies another Royalist's recollection, that of Sir Philip Warwick, who remembered how, as a young, courtly dandy, he came across the plain-dressed, plain-speaking Cromwell in the House of Commons.

I came into the House well clad and perceived a gentleman speaking (whom I knew not) very ordinary apparelled, for it was a plain cloth-sute, which seemed to have bin made by an ill country taylor; his linen was plain, and not very clean; and I remember a speck or two of blood upon his little band which was not much bigger than his collar, his hatt was without a hatband ... his countenance swollen and red-dich, his voice sharp and untunable, and his eloquence full of fervour; for the subject matter could not bear much of reason.[5]

On other occasions in his *Memoirs*, Warwick recounts stories from third parties of Cromwell's hypochondria and dissolute 'gaming' life before his 'conversion', but here is a first-hand (if admittedly retrospective) picture both of his appearance, and, more reliably, the traits for which he would become well known: plainness, irascibility and a refusal to stand on ceremony. The record of Cromwell's participation in numerous aspects of parliamentary business, from moving readings of bills to telling votes, shows that he was very far from Puritan Junto 'lobby fodder', and these intimations of self-possession and an unwillingness to allow form to trump argument fit well with this picture.

After the air of crisis was exacerbated by the outbreak of rebellion in Ireland in October 1641, Cromwell continued to place himself where he could be useful to the godly. The Catholic Irish insurgency was accompanied by stories of atrocities on both sides, and a claim that it was backed by Charles I, a rumour promoted by the Irish leader of the rebellion with an almost certainly forged document. The twinning of anti-popery with anti-royalism, which the king's marriage to a Catholic and promotion of a form of Protestant worship associated with Catholicism had long made possible, was all but sealed by these developments. Rumours of a 'popish plot' took hold, and Charles was led to believe that Parliament intended to arrest his queen, Henrietta Maria, for her (alleged) part in it. It was in reaction to this apparent threat that Charles issued his famous warrant for the arrest on treason charges of the six members in January 1642 – five from the House of Commons, including Pym and Hampden, and one from the Lords, Viscount Mandeville (Edward Montagu, the future Earl of Manchester, with whom, despite their shared politics, Cromwell had clashed more than once, including at Hyde's committee, and would clash again).

On 4 January 1642, Charles arrived at the House of Commons in person, with as many as 500 troops in tow, to take the five MPs into custody himself, only to find that, forewarned, they had already slipped away. Such was the drama of the occasion that the Commons *Journal* broke off its account. So it is to the recollections of the Commons clerk-assistant John Rushworth, written in the 1650s, that we owe the king's famous observation from the Speaker's chair, 'I see all the Birds are flown.'[6] Charles's bungled invasion of the Commons was the symbolic moment at which trust between the king and Parliament irrevocably broke down. As the king left the chamber in humiliation, Cromwell would have been among the members who shouted 'Privilege! Privilege!' at his back. The next day, the House issued a Vindication of the 'high Breach of the Rights and Privilege of Parliament', vocally demonstrating that it was not only the king whose honour could be offended.[7] But the breakdown was far more than rhetorical, and in the following months Cromwell played his part as Parliament made preparations for war, including a small role in initiating the Militia Ordinance. Beginning life as a Militia Bill, it was renamed an ordinance when the king refused to assent to it: the ordinance was a crucial step on the way to war, giving Parliament authority to raise their own forces and appoint Lords Lieutenant. As well as a practical measure for parliamentary defence, it was the clearest usurpation yet of a role traditionally reserved to the crown, of raising forces for the defence of the realm. The king duly used another mechanism, the (medieval) commission of array, to summon his own forces. On Parliament's side, the Earl of Essex was appointed as Lord General of the Army. In July 1642 Charles, who had abandoned London when opinion seemed to be running high against him (another tactical blunder, to set alongside the provocation of the Scots and the bungled arrest of the five members, among many), issued requests to Oxford and Cambridge Universities to send their college plate to him in York, to help his finances. Oxford obliged, but Cromwell, as MP for Cambridge, was an obvious candidate to persuade his old university not to follow suit. He set out in August 1642 from London for his constituency, gathering a small armed force on the way.

Cromwell's march to Cambridge was the first action in what became one of the most extraordinary military careers of any Englishman. Like almost all his comrades, Cromwell took up arms against the king not to remove him, still less to remove kingship itself, but – as so many of those who had opposed their sovereign over centuries of English history had done before – to bring the king back into the way of good government, and to remove those around him who were leading him astray. All this had happened before, and while civil war remained a last resort, it was one that English subjects had reached on numerous occasions. But the scale and extent of this civil war were unprecedented, as were the eventual casualties. It was in part because the cost became so great that the war came to have such profound consequences. But for Oliver, as for the country, it was only much later that more radical, indeed revolutionary, steps were contemplated.

3
'Valiant Colonel Cromwell'

Oliver Cromwell's military deeds raised him to national attention. His fame sprang mostly from his own achievements, but from early on he was alive to the chances of self-promotion – which, no doubt, he would have viewed as the promotion of his cause – and to the importance of imposing his view of events on others. The great explosion in pamphlet and newsbook printing of the seventeenth century was set off when Parliament removed restrictions on publishing that had been imposed by Charles I's government. Later, when in power, Cromwell, like Charles, would be moved to suppress unpalatable reporting; during his rise to power, however, he benefited from press freedom. Along with his fellow Parliamentarians, such as Sir Thomas Fairfax, John Pym and Robert Devereux, the Earl of Essex, Cromwell would also become a familiar face across the country, his image appearing in engravings circulated during the war.

While Cromwell's trajectory from gentleman to ruler was unprecedented in English history, it was preceded by a scarcely less unusual ascent to popular fame – or notoriety, as far as his enemies were concerned. Charles I, it has often been pointed out, was attempting to promote the sacredness of kingship at a time when popular prints were engaged in 'desacralizing' royalty. But pamphlets, news-books and engravings could all be used to bolster images too: posthumously, with the publication of the wildly successful *Eikon Basilike*, a humble defence of the king's actions purportedly written in his own words, the phenomenon benefited Charles more than it ever had in his lifetime. On Parliament's side, there were several stars in the early part of the war, notably William Waller, whose successes in the south-east made him 'William the Conqueror' in the parliamentary press. No one, however, rode the wave of press and public opinion in the 1640s and 1650s to more personal benefit than Oliver Cromwell.

At the beginning of his parliamentary career, Cromwell had found himself among more experienced politicians and better speakers who naturally took the lead. In the parliamentary army, too, Cromwell began as a minor figure. From early on, though, the confusions of war provided him with the chance to think on his feet, and to put his personal decisions more often into action than he could in the Commons. His first command was only a partial success. By the time he arrived in Cambridge, leading a small force tasked with preventing the despatch of college plate to the king, some silver had already been spirited away. But Cromwell reacted quickly, securing the plate in the remaining colleges, and taking possession of the magazine at Cambridge Castle. No shots were fired or blows exchanged, though armed representatives of both town and university turned out for the king. Among them was Cromwell's cousin, his uncle Sir Oliver's son Henry. Cromwell's own son and namesake was a Cambridge undergraduate who did support his father's cause, and later served as a captain of horse under him. Although not everything had gone to plan, Cromwell had shown he could be relied upon. Shortly after, he returned briefly to Parliament to receive its thanks, before making his way to Huntingdon, where he set about raising a troop of horse.

There were no professional armies in England at the outbreak of the Civil War, but there were men with military experience. More of these were on the Royalist side, including the king's nephews the Rhine Princes Rupert and Maurice, sons of the Elector of the Rhine Palatinate Frederick V: they had seen action on the continent in the Dutch Revolt and the Thirty Years War. Lord Fairfax and his son Sir Thomas were among the parliamentary commanders who had served abroad, also fighting for the Dutch Protestants. Cromwell was in the majority who had never fought – but not many of his contemporaries learned faster. That included two future commanders on either side: the Earl of Manchester, who became major-general in the Eastern Association of counties in 1643, and Cromwell's commanding officer, and the Earl (later Marquess) of Newcastle, who commanded the Royalist forces in the north. To begin with, however, Cromwell's education was less a matter of strategy and tactics than of recruitment and fundraising for the parliamentary cause.

At the outbreak of war, the country was not neatly divided between Parliament and king. The king's main areas of loyalty were in the north and parts of the west, including Cornwall and most of Wales, while Parliament could rely on London and the east, with three fingers of parliamentary land stretching north and westwards, up to Hull, into Lancashire and across towards Bristol and Gloucester. Strategically, it was clear that the Royalists would attempt to squeeze Parliament from the north and west, while Parliament would try to expand its territory into the same areas. The two external factors – of potential Irish reinforcements for Charles if the rebellion there could be quieted, and, on the Parliamentarian side, potential Scottish aid if some agreement between Covenanters and Parliament could be reached – would also be crucial. But within these areas, and especially on their edges, loyalties were unpredictable, and the support of different communities was often hard won.

Cromwell's certainty of the rightness of his cause, and the furious energy with which he approached the business of recruitment and fundraising, were among the qualities that made him an outstanding officer in these circumstances. They were certainly as important as the tactical and strategic lessons he assimilated with extraordinary speed from the experience of actual combat. His rise and eventual eminence were part of a process that ensured that the more 'radical' positions he represented – on not compromising with the king; on the importance of reforming religion and morals, though not necessarily, as his opponents alleged, on a broader 'levelling' of society – all came to the fore as the Civil War turned into a revolution.

Later, as Lord Protector, Cromwell gave an account of his own theories of recruitment, as well as an insight into his rapid promotion: 'I was a person that from my first employment was suddenly preferred and lifted up from lesser trusts to greater, from my first being a captain of troop of horse. And I did labour as well as I could to discharge my trust, and God blessed me as it pleased him.' One of the first problems he identified was with the quality and commitment of the troops Parliament was raising to fight its wars. He recalled addressing his cousin John Hampden, probably just after the first major encounter of the war, the Battle of Edgehill, about reinforcing the Parliamentarian army: 'Your troopers, said I, are most of them old decayed serving men and tapsters, and such kind of fellows, and, said I, their [the Royalists'] troopers are gentlemen's sons, younger sons, persons of quality: do you think that the spirits of such base and mean fellows will ever be able to encounter gentlemen that have honour, courage and resolution in them? . . . You must get men of a spirit . . . that is like to go as far as a gentleman will go, or else I am sure you will be beaten still.'

There is no reason to suppose that Cromwell was embellishing his recollection much. From our first view of him, he had always been ready to voice his opinion even to, or perhaps especially to, someone he respected as 'a wise and worthy person'. Hampden thought the notion of restricting recruitment to 'spirited' men impractical when numbers seemed all-important, but Cromwell 'raised such men as had the fear of God before them, and made some conscience of what they did. And from that day forward they were never beaten.'[1] His sometimes desperate pleas for troops throughout the year 1643 still usually prized quality over quantity: 'I beseech you be careful what captains of horse you choose, what men be mounted; a few honest men are better than numbers . . . If you choose godly honest men . . . honest men will follow them.'[2]

The recruiting principle that associated military capability with conspicuous godliness anticipated the later formation of Parliament's New Model Army. It was a principle that brought Cromwell success, celebrity, controversy and opprobrium in almost equal measure, as the way the war was fought, to what end and for whose benefit all came into contention over the following four years and beyond. Cromwell's epiphany about recruitment came after his first experience of combat, which was hardly auspicious. At the first pitched battle of the Civil War, the confused, bloody and inconclusive engagement on 23 October 1642 between the king and Essex's Parliamentarian army at Edgehill in Warwickshire, Cromwell's troop seems to have arrived late, as did Hampden's brigade. They did little to affect the outcome. But if neither side could claim victory, the Royalists were, crucially, not prevented from continuing towards London. Cromwell may have been part of the hastily assembled force, including the London trained bands and those of Hertfordshire, Essex and Surrey, that turned out to repel Charles's rapid advance on the capital at Turnham Green. If so, he was present at an occasion where, for the first time, large numbers of volunteers showed the wider popularity of Parliament's cause, along with the sort of 'spirit' that Cromwell was searching for, in a stand-off that was as important as any deadlier engagement of the Civil War. There was a lot of fighting after Turnham Green, but it would turn out to have been the king's best chance of winning the war quickly.

If Charles were to lose it, however, Parliament would have to make him do so slowly. That was one implication of Manchester's remark to Cromwell in 1644: 'If we beat the King 99 times, yet he is King still.'[3] The other was, of course, that whatever the military outcome of the war, Parliament would still have to decide how to deal with the king, whose status couldn't be altered by something as ephemeral as a lost battle.

In the first year of the war, although Cromwell had more success in a hard campaign for Parliament than many of his comrades, beating the king even once proved difficult. Cromwell's early contribution to an increasingly attritional conflict was made on home territory, in the fenlands around the Isle of Ely, before he was sent north into Lincolnshire and Nottinghamshire. In early 1643, he had impressed the parliamentary authorities enough to receive a promotion, from captain to colonel, in command of a regiment of horse under the new eastern counties' major-general, William, Lord Grey of Warke. In the course of the year, while Grey himself was absent assisting the Earl of Essex besieging Reading, Cromwell took effective command of the eastern counties, concentrating his efforts on the defence of Ely, as well as action in Lowestoft, King's Lynn, Peterborough and, in April that year, the bombardment of Crowland Abbey. In July he led his cavalry to the capture of Burghley House and the relief of the Lincolnshire manor of Gainsborough.

He began to appear in the parliamentary press as 'valiant Colonell Cromwell': a singling-out that he no doubt attributed to Providence, but which would, a year later, form a portion of the charge against him made by an anonymous 'opponent', who alleged that the valiant colonel was in fact one of those men who 'gloryes in themselves whilst we have warre'. The same anonymous accuser charged Cromwell with taking the credit for other men's deeds (such as those of the 'opponent' himself): 'that servisse, and all other done by me and others, must goe in his name or ells alls was not well'.[4] Whatever the motivation for such criticism, or the truth behind it, it demonstrated two things. First, that Cromwell, now clearly on the up, would cause resentment. Secondly, that resentment was unlikely to blow him off course.

Cromwell's first success in a pitched battle, for which again he seems to have received more than his fair share of credit, was at Winceby, Lincolnshire, in October 1643. During the initial cavalry charge his horse was shot from under him. Remounting, he and his cavalry 'performed with so much admirable courage and resolution ... that the Enemy stood not another'.[5] This breathless account, which also relates how the Parliamentarians marched to war singing psalms, may be doing his fellow cavalry commander Sir Thomas Fairfax's contribution to winning the fight a disservice. Another parliamentary paper depicted 'that Noble Sir Thomas Fairfax' (who had far more military experience than Cromwell) as relishing being outnumbered: 'I never prospered better,' he reportedly said, 'than when I fought against the Enemy three or four to one.'[6]

It was understandable that Parliament's supporters should make so much of a relatively small engagement, and the commanders who delivered victory. Elsewhere that year, the war was not going well for them. Royalist gains in the north and west even encouraged a tentative round of peace negotiations, though both sides' starting positions were much too far apart for those to have any real prospect of success. For Cromwell, however, the year ended with more good news. He was promoted to the rank of lieutenant-general, below the Earl of Manchester, who had replaced Grey as General of the Eastern Association. That December, the map of England showed big gains for the Royalists: both in the west, where Parliament was reduced to isolated strongholds at Plymouth, Gloucester and Pembroke; and in the Midlands, where Cromwell's contribution had merely been as part of an effort to resist further encroachment. What is more, in a move that shocked Protestant opinion but added to Royalist manpower, Charles I agreed a cessation of hostilities with the Irish rebels, thereby freeing up troops, many of them Catholic, to come over to England to aid his cause.

In September 1643, after long negotiation (John Pym's last great achievement before his death at the end of the year), Parliament managed to secure its own external help, which was to prove vital to winning the war, but also played a pivotal role in the course of the subsequent peace: they agreed to join forces with the Presbyterian Scottish Covenanters. The price for Scottish cooperation (the price apart from money, that is) was parliamentary agreement to the Solemn League and Covenant hammered out between the allies, which committed Parliament to imposing Presbyterianism in all three kingdoms. The letter of the agreement may not have spelled this out, but as it talked of 'preserving' Scottish religion (i.e. Presbyterianism) and 'reforming' English and Irish, the implication was clear. The Covenanters went on to provide 20,000 troops to the cause, troops who in their effectiveness and numerical superiority far outweighed the king's Irish auxiliaries. Perhaps the most serious consequence of Charles's decision was to give ammunition to those who saw the Royalists as crypto-Catholics, and their ultimate goal as the one that some had feared all along: 'the malignant design, now in hand by force of arms to hinder reformation of religion and church government and to introduce popery and suspicion'. Or, in other words, to return England to Catholicism.[7]

On 5 February 1644 Cromwell belatedly signed the Solemn League and Covenant in person on a rare return to Parliament. He was also appointed to the Committee of Both Kingdoms, which from now on would direct the parliamentary effort in the war. Although Cromwell thus made the same commitment as Parliament now required from every loyal Englishman over the age of eighteen, his own religious position was set against Presbyterianism, preferring the less formal organization based on gathered congregations of like minds known as Independency. Consequently, he may, in private, have been reluctant to take the Covenant. But it is likely that he was in sympathy with the spirit, if not the letter, of the oath, which talked of 'our unfeigned desire to be humbled for our sins and for the sins of these kingdoms; especially that we have not as

we ought valued the inestimable value of the Gospel'.[8]
There were always divisions in the alliances that fought
against Charles, but there were powerful forces bringing
them together: to Cromwell, as to so many of his contemporaries, nothing was more urgent in that regard than the
word of God – 'quick, and powerful, and sharper than any
two-edged sword', as the New Testament put it, in words
that would have been very familiar to the godly majority,
for whom Bible-reading was a cornerstone of worship.[9]

On Cromwell's return to action in February 1644, he
had some success in Buckinghamshire and Lincolnshire
before marching north with Manchester's army to join
Lord Fairfax and his son Sir Thomas, and Parliament's
new Scottish allies under the Earl of Leven, following
which this combined force laid siege to the Marquess of
Newcastle at York, a siege raised when Prince Rupert
approached with his army. Precipitately, Rupert then pursued the retreating Parliamentarians, who turned to face
him at Tadcaster. Rupert's impetuosity became a feature
of the fighting, his cavalry's indiscipline contrasting with
the obedience of Cromwell's.

On 2 July 1644 the two armies, Rupert now joined by
Newcastle, clashed at Marston Moor. It was the biggest
and deadliest battle of the war. On Parliament's side,
Cromwell's horse on the left and Sir Thomas Fairfax's on
the right flanked the infantry of Manchester, Lord Fairfax
and Parliament's overall commander, Leven. These allied
Parliamentarian forces outnumbered their opponents by
perhaps 28,000 to 18,000, but the battle was still close-
run. Both Thomas Fairfax and Cromwell were wounded,

Cromwell leaving the battle for a while to have his wound dressed. But, after the Royalists had initially broken through on the other side while Cromwell was being treated, he returned to ensure that it was on his flank that the battle turned in Parliament's favour. Cromwell's cavalry were able to counter-attack and, as he famously wrote afterwards, 'God made them as stubble to our swords.' Not all the casualties were on one side, however, as the same letter, written to his brother-in-law Valentine Walton, makes painfully clear.

The ominous tenor of the opening – 'It's our duty to sympathise in all mercies that we praise the Lord together in chastisement or trials, so that we may sorrow together' – is put to one side for an account of Parliament's 'absolute victory'. But then comes the news that 'God hath taken away your eldest son by cannon-shot'. The offered consolation is, of course, eternal: 'Sir, you know my trial this way' – Cromwell had lost his own eldest son Oliver to smallpox just over three months before – 'but the Lord supported me with this: that the Lord took him into the happiness we all pant after and live for. There is your precious child full of glory, to know sin nor sorrow any more. He was a gallant young man, exceeding gracious. God give you His comfort.'[10] On the Royalist side, the death toll was more than ten times the 300 Parliamentarian dead: 4,150 died, among them all but thirty of Newcastle's 3,000 Whitecoats Regiment, who refused quarter.

After this disaster, Newcastle himself was less obdurate. He went into exile in the Netherlands, playing no further part in the war. His reason for doing so sheds more light on the mixture of motivations and concerns that moved men to fight or not to fight in the times: loss of face. Newcastle could not 'endure the laughter of the court'.[11] Such courtly, aristocratic *amour propre* was a world away from the atmosphere of determined, almost fanatical commitment in which Cromwell operated. It was also, of course, a Royalist world, but one wonders if the increasing signs of discontent with Parliament's own lordly commanders that took hold from around this time contained a suspicion that, for all their differences, Parliament's peers shared something of the attitudes and culture of the men they were meant to defeat. If so, they might be more inclined to treat with their opposite numbers, rather than pressing their advantage. It is difficult to sustain the argument that Cromwell and those who shared his religious and political outlook necessarily had any social 'levelling' agenda, something they were accused of at the time. But, as the detailed business of war strategy and war aims began to dominate parliamentary discussions, now conducted under the aegis of the Committee of Both Kingdoms, there is a sense that the Commons, however disunited they were among themselves, began to believe they had a monopoly on the genuine parliamentary cause.

These divisions became more overt because Marston Moor turned out not to be the decisive victory that Parliament's supporters hoped. To begin with, opinion differed over who should take credit for it. Cromwell had written to Walton that 'The left wing, which I commanded, being our own horse, save a few Scots in the rear, beat all the

Prince's horse.' This was in stark contrast to Scottish views of the battle, for example that of the minister Robert Baillie, who wrote that David Leslie, the Scottish cavalry commander who had supported Cromwell's horse, 'in all places that day was his [Cromwell's] leader', and that reports of the battle 'give much more to Cromwell than we are informed is his due'.[12] It must have been true at the very least that Leslie and the Scottish contingent held their own while Cromwell was away from the battlefield for medical treatment.

Though in his private letter Cromwell included the characteristic imperative – 'Give glory, all the glory, to God' – the belittling of the Scots' contribution was a manifestation of existing tensions between the English and Scottish causes. He had twice clashed with the Scottish major-general Lawrence Crawford, who had wanted to dismiss an officer of Cromwell's for his religious opinions. Cromwell defended the officer in strikingly modern terms: 'the State, in choosing men to serve them, takes no notice of their opinions'.[13] However laudable the sentiment to our ears, though, this was simply untrue. The Solemn League and Covenant, to which the offending officer, like all adult males, was compelled to swear, did indeed take notice of opinions. If a man felt conscientiously unable to sign it, he could hardly serve in Parliament's army. As always with Cromwell, it is impossible to know whether to take his argument at face value. Even after he rose to power, he agonized greatly over liberty for 'tender' religious consciences, so it must be admitted that this argument was part of a consistent outlook. Then again, Cromwell was known to be a popular and charismatic leader, who recruited among Independents. This was his own preference. So his defence of his man against Crawford is also a straightforward objection to another commander, and a Scottish Presbyterian, interfering in what Cromwell clearly thought of as his own business. The passion and consistency with which, here as so often, Cromwell embraced a principled argument should not be permitted to conceal the fact that there were personal issues at stake too.

Disagreeing over who should take credit for a great victory was one thing. Failing to capitalize on that victory was far worse. Yet, through a series of strategic and tactical blunders, some of which may have betrayed an attitude to war aims that differed greatly from Cromwell's, that is what Parliament and their allies did after Marston Moor. Cromwell was not implicated in most of these setbacks, something which was to prove significant later on. The first came when the commander-in-chief of Parliament's forces, the Earl of Essex, who had been conducting a campaign in the west of England, was lured into chasing a Royalist army deep into Cornwall, while another Royalist force under the king sealed off his route back. At Lostwithiel on 2 September 1644 Essex's infantry surrendered, while the Lord General himself got away by ship.

This was a setback for Parliament, but not a fatal one. They regrouped, and a combined army led by Manchester (with Cromwell), Essex and Waller (the south-eastern major-general who was at loggerheads with Essex) faced a Royalist army, which had turned eastwards, at Newbury on 27 October 1644, the second time battle had been joined there in the Civil War. Before this battle, Cromwell had been engaged in a series of attacks on Royalist bases around Oxford. He had also taken the time to appear before Parliament and formally demand Crawford's removal as major-general, though he was persuaded to withdraw that ultimatum. During this time, he was becoming involved in another increasingly heated dispute with the Presbyterian Earl of Manchester, whose desultory contribution to the campaign between Marston Moor and Newbury exasperated his lieutenant-general.

When Manchester and Cromwell fought side by side again at Newbury, however, it was Cromwell whose inexplicably slow reactions failed to clinch the potential Parliamentarian triumph, when one flank of the king's forces was routed in a complex engagement. Cromwell hesitated, and his cavalry on the other flank was charged by his Royalist opposite number, Lord Goring. Although neither side could claim victory after this Second Battle of Newbury, the fact that the Royalists were able to reach Oxford unmolested made it more of a frustration for Parliament, on whom the onus remained to achieve a decisive, concluding triumph. It is in this context that Manchester made his remark about defeating the king ninety-nine times, 'yet he is King still'. For Cromwell, this was a counsel of despair: 'If this be so, why did we take up arms at first? This is against fighting ever hereafter.'[14] But Manchester had a point, if Parliament were unable to press home its advantages. It was the fundamental point at the heart of any attempt to challenge the will of the king. What constituted success? If the answer was to have the king at your mercy, how could the victors impose their terms reliably and still allow Charles to remain on the throne? For the time being, however, Parliament needed to find a way to make its military advantages count. Cromwell and like-minded MPs suspected that Manchester was more unwilling than unable to make sure that happened. Despite the fact that Cromwell's own shortcomings at the Battle of Newbury were at least as open to criticism as any of Manchester's there, it was after Newbury that Cromwell brought his suspicions before the House of Commons, in November 1644:

> I thought the Earl of Manchester was most in fault for most of these miscarriages and the ill consequences of them. And because I had a great deal of reason to think that his Lordship's miscarriage in these particulars was neither through accidents (which could not be helped) nor through his improvidence only, but through backwardness to all action, and had some reason to conceive that that backwardness was not (merely) from dullness or indisposedness to engagement, but (withal) from some principle of unwillingness in his Lordship to have this war prosecuted unto a full victory, and a design or desire to have it ended by accommodation (and that) on some such terms to which it might be disadvantageous to bring the King too low.[15]

With this, and his references to Manchester's 'shuffling pretences and evasions', Cromwell was effectively accusing his commanding officer of treason: alleging not just that he had failed Parliament but that he had done so deliberately, and underhandedly, in order to help the enemy, 'contrary to commands received', to such an extent that 'he had seemed studiously to decline the gaining of such advantages upon the enemy'. The usual name given to this episode, 'the quarrel between Manchester and Cromwell', makes it sound a rather low-temperature contest. In fact, both men's reputations, their futures and, in Manchester's case, given the severity of Cromwell's accusations, potentially his life, were at stake. While this 'quarrel' was being aired, two prisoners in the Tower, John Hotham father and son, were awaiting their fate having been arrested for going over to the Royalists (Hotham senior had been the Governor of Hull, whose refusal of entry to Charles was one of the first hostile acts of the Civil Wars). In January 1645, both were beheaded.

In the circumstances, it is no wonder that Manchester went on the offensive himself, alleging that Cromwell packed his troops of horse with sectaries, followers of radical and potentially revolutionary Protestant teaching. In the words of the anonymous 'opponent', who had served with Cromwell at the beginning of the war, and who also supplied evidence to the committee appointed to resolve the dispute, Cromwell was reported to have said that 'God would have noe lording over his peopell, and he verily believed that God would sweep away that lord in power out of this nation'.[16] To Cromwell's accusation that Manchester had not been vigorous enough in his pursuit of Charles, Manchester hit back with the opposite: that, contrary to the stated war aims of Parliament, which had never been to remove Charles, Cromwell was scheming for just that.

This episode might be taken as another example of Oliver's impetuosity, and his inability to cooperate with his superiors if he believed they were in the wrong: neither quality recommends itself as one for a successful soldier or politician. However, the outcome of the quarrel points to something different. Cromwell won: the Commons Committee for the Army, which had heard the dispute, endorsed his criticisms of Manchester on 9 December. To get that favourable verdict, Cromwell had built up a powerful coalition of supporters, not all of whom were natural allies. They included the chairman of the committee, Zouch Tate, a Presbyterian MP.

The debate that followed the committee's endorsement showed that Tate and Cromwell had found a way of working together. Cromwell outlined the popular notion that Parliament was failing to win the war because it was no longer in the personal interests of Parliamentarian commanders to do so. 'Members of both Houses hath got great places and commands, and . . . will perpetually continue themselves in grandeur, and not permit the War speedily to end.' Tate followed him by proposing that 'during the time of the war, no member of either House shall have or execute any office or command'.[17] This proposal led to the Self-Denying Ordinance, which established the complete separation of Parliament and its armies – meaning that no longer could peers such as Manchester command Parliamentarian forces. It was clearly not a spontaneous move; the trio of Cromwell, Tate and Cromwell's fellow Independent Sir Henry Vane speaking to the same theme one after the other had the hoped-for effect of carrying first the Commons, and eventually the Lords with them.

The Self-Denying Ordinance solved Parliament's and Cromwell's difficulties with the dubious leadership of peers such as Essex and Manchester. But it also created a problem for Cromwell himself – who, as MP for Cambridge, should, like them, have been excluded from military command. It is impossible to know whether Cromwell expected or planned for the eventual solution, which was to exempt him, if only temporarily and over some objections, from the ordinance, allowing him to resume his post. It is, however, eloquent witness to Cromwell's own rise that, barely two years after he had first taken up arms, the country gentleman from Huntingdon (who could, after all, have stood down from his parliamentary seat) was deemed indispensable to Parliament's cause, while traditional leaders from the aristocracy (who could not resign their places in the Lords) had apparently become redundant.

The issue of the prosecution of the war was a wider one for Parliament than the dispute between two of its commanders. But it would become typical of Oliver that his personal troubles became inextricable from the nation's, and that the solution to them was a change in national policy, rather than a mere alteration in individual circumstances. This link between one man's personality and the direction of the nation is one with which we are familiar when dealing with monarchs, and occasionally with great nobles. Cromwell is the first commoner to have made the same connection. What people call greatness can often be found to lie in the extent to which a person can involve others in the drama of their lives, and persuade the public of the importance for them of the fortunes of one individual. By that measure, Oliver Cromwell was beginning to be a great man.

It was not only issues of command, or indeed will to win (or lack of it), that had made Parliament incapable of pressing home their undoubted advantages in men and resources. It was also problems in the army's structure and organization. The solution to these problems, proposed in January 1645, was the 'new modelling' of the army. Though some regional forces remained, and the Scots continued with a separate army in the field, the New Model became Parliament's main instrument for winning the war. Answerable directly to the Committee of Both Kingdoms, it would at its envisaged full strength be a powerful force of 6,000 horse, 14,400 foot and 1,000 dragoons (mounted infantry). It began to be formed from February 1645, even before legislation had passed both Houses. It was to be paid for in a far more regulated way than previous armies, which had existed almost hand to mouth, with an assessment of £56,000 to be drawn from all parliamentary regions.

Cromwell was deeply involved in the committees to set up the New Model Army, though until his own position was resolved he could not, of course, expect to serve in it. He supported the appointment of Sir Thomas Fairfax as Lord General, and of Philip Skippon, an experienced soldier who had endured difficult service under Essex, as sergeant-major-general. The fact that the post of lieutenant-general went conspicuously unfilled surely suggests that Cromwell had hopes, if not expectations, of an exemption from the Self-Denying Ordinance. When, the following May, Leicester fell to Prince Rupert's Royalist troops, the crisis was acute enough for Cromwell to be appointed as lieutenant-general. The appointment was never permanent, and was repeatedly renewed during the rest of the war, a reminder that Cromwell remained an exception to the rule he had helped to create, that his rise to supremacy rested on a technicality.

The campaign that eventually brought Parliament lasting victory had begun in May 1645 with Fairfax, his force still at half-strength, besieging Oxford, but the sack of Leicester had the intended effect of drawing the New Model Army away from the king's capital. Fairfax requested Cromwell's appointment as lieutenant-general, in command of the horse, and though the Lords refused, the Commons assented, their endorsement apparently sufficient in the circumstances. Marching from Ely, where he had been raising troops, to Fairfax's army in Leicestershire, Cromwell was 'received with the greatest joy', and the following day, at Naseby near Market Harborough, he commanded the right wing of the army with Henry Ireton on the left and Skippon in the centre.

At Naseby, on 14 June 1645, Cromwell's contribution was perhaps his most important to date, as the discipline of his cavalry rescued a perilous position and kept his horse together on the field, where they overwhelmed the cavalry and then the infantry of their opponents. Parliament outnumbered the Royalists by around 15,000 to 8,000, but those numbers could only be brought to bear if they stayed united on the battlefield. Once again, as at York, Rupert's cavalry could not be prevented from pursuing the enemy off the field, while Cromwell kept his horse intact, and was able to turn it decisively against the

Royalist foot, unprotected in the centre. The result was a total victory for the New Model Army in its first battle, with 1,000 Royalist dead and 4,500 prisoners taken, compared to around 200 dead on Parliament's side.

Cromwell naturally saw 'the good hand of God' at Naseby, and praised his general Fairfax as well as the troops. But others were happy to give the new lieutenant-general the credit: 'Cromwell charging before them, with his Horse brake into the Kings Body, routed them, ceized up on all their Train and Canon, took 4,000 Foot and Horse prisoners, their Standard, Engines, 70 carriages, 12 pieces of Ordnance . . . took the Kings own Waggons, and in one of them a Cabinet of Letters supposed to be of great consequence.'[18] Cromwell's own report of the battle reached Parliament before Fairfax's, and he took the opportunity of manipulating the moral of the victory: 'honest men served you faithfully in this action. Sir, they are trusty; I beseech you in the name of God, not to discourage them . . . He that ventures his life for the liberty of this country, I wish he trust God for the liberty of his conscience, and you for the liberty he fights for.'[19]Although the Commons took out this final plea from the published version of the letter, as they would do with subsequent pleas on the same lines, the Lords' publication didn't, so that Cromwell's association of victory at Naseby with the cause of liberty of conscience – and against the strict imposition of Presbyterianism implied by the Solemn League and Covenant that many in Parliament still hoped for – would not be forgotten.

*

Over the next eleven months, a far more effective and vigorous campaign to capitalize on Parliament's victory at
Naseby played out than had followed Marston Moor. As
the Royalists were squeezed ever harder, and ultimate
victory approached, Cromwell continued to make pleas
for the case that a religious settlement should not be
imposed, that all good Protestants should be accommo-
dated in the future. In arms, 'Presbyterians, Independents,
all had the same spirit of faith and prayer ... they agree
here, know no names of difference: pity it is it should be
otherwise anywhere.'[20] Parliament, where Presbyterians
dominated, continued to suppress such outpourings, but
they were distributed in pamphlet form anyway. Cromwell's successes during this campaign – with and without
Fairfax – at Langport, Bristol, Winchester and Basing
House were part of a summer and autumn of Parliamentarian progress that tightened the noose around the
Royalist cause.

Though Charles held out until the new year, hoped-for
relief from Scottish supporters under the Marquis of Mon-
trose or a new injection of Irish manpower came to
nothing. As Fairfax besieged Oxford in April 1646, Cromwell briefly returned to Parliament. By the time he joined
the siege, Charles had already escaped, making his way to
Southwell to surrender to the Scots on 5 May. It was the
king's final manoeuvre in a strategy that had long relied on
seeking weaknesses in the parliamentary alliance. That he
thought he was likely to do better in Scottish hands than
English may have had something to do with the growing
perception that the more 'Radical' Parliamentarians, of

whom Cromwell was now the most celebrated, had acquired the loudest voice among Charles's enemies. Whether or not that judgement reflected reality, the king was surely right to assume that at this point, with the triumphs of the New Model Army still fresh, Parliament could not be relied upon to offer Charles the terms on which he had surrendered to David Leslie: not to make him go against his conscience, and to support him if Parliament refused to reinstate his rights and prerogatives. There were many MPs who had long since rejected that as a basis for accommodation. Cromwell was one of them.

4
General and Regicide

Cromwell was almost the only man, and certainly the most prominent, who remained an MP and a serving officer in this period of the Civil War. That put him in a unique position to influence the next phase of events. It can be tempting to cast the time up to the execution of the king in January 1649 as the latest stage in Oliver's inexorable rise to pre-eminence. And yet, although he certainly did emerge during these years as one of the most important voices, and the most effective commander in the country, the process looks anything but inexorable. In the confusion generated by the end of the war, which came after Charles's surrender in May 1646 – what with the criss-crossing arguments of the king, his supporters, Presbyterians and Independents in Parliament, the Scots Covenanters, political radicals and the simply ill-treated in the army, and those inside and outside both Houses who wanted to seek more agreeable terms with Charles – Cromwell was often to be found attempting a balancing act between at least two bodies of opinion. In particular, his loyalty to Parliament and his loyalty to the army became, if not mutually exclusive, at least incompatible. Now that Charles was defeated, Cromwell's two masters' differences, in religion and political outlook, emerged more starkly. Partly in consequence, with his growing fame came growing censure from all sides. One of the most persistent accusations against him was one of hypocrisy: his desire to find a solution, willingness to listen to arguments, but ultimate intransigence on matters closest to his conscience all combined to give the impression that he was disingenuous. Charles was accused of much the same: in his case, though, his own private correspondence reveals the allegations to be well founded. The personal motivations in Cromwell's surviving private correspondence are, however, not as easy to pin down, or expose. Cromwell could always argue that his actions were guided by a concern to follow the promptings of Providence, and the mind of the Lord. Many of his letters from this period reveal an agonized attempt to discern what that was. If the results were mysterious to some, that was the way the Lord moved.

Comparing Cromwell and the king can be misleading, if it tempts us to think of the two as having anything like equal weight for their respective sides at this time. While Charles indisputably still spoke for his party, despite his defeat and capture, Cromwell was only one of many speakers on his side. Indeed, the most noticeable thing about Cromwell in the first part of the process to extricate the king from Scottish control and impose mutually acceptable terms on him is how unnoticeable he was. The MP for Cambridge resumed his place on numerous parliamentary committees and was the teller in numerous votes. But anyone unaware of his record or his future who

analysed the months between Charles's surrender to the
Scots in 1646 and the crisis precipitated by the break
between the army and Parliament the following year would
be unlikely to make him out as the key player. In simple
terms, this was because the group of Independents with
which he was increasingly associated were not in the
majority in either House. In any case, even among the
Independents, Cromwell was not yet the leading parliamentary voice. Arguably, he never became so: almost all
his really significant political interventions came in spite
of, rather than because of, his parliamentary connection.
The driving Independent force in the Commons was Sir
Henry Vane, known as the Younger to distinguish him
from his father, who had played a major role in the fall of
the Earl of Strafford, but was now eclipsed by his more
uncompromising son. The other leader of the Independents in the Commons was Cromwell's brother-in-law,
Oliver St John, although, like Cromwell, he played a
quieter role during this period. On the Presbyterian side –
those whose religious views made them more natural
allies of the Scots – with the majority of MPs behind him
was Denzil Holles, who had long favoured making terms
with Charles, and now sought a wholesale demilitariza-
tion on all sides: Royalists, Scots and, most troublesomely,
the New Model Army.

The only part of Holles's plan that worked was the
removal of the Scots, whom Parliament in effect paid to
hand over Charles and go home. In February 1647, after
two down-payments totalling £200,000, the king was surrendered to Parliament and kept in captivity at Holmby

House in Northamptonshire. Cromwell was a signatory to the agreement with the Scots – but he had not negotiated it. Indeed, in the same month, a Royalist intelligence report informed Edward Hyde that 'Cromwell is dangerously ill'.

It was given out that he had 'an imposthume [abscess] in the head', something that, it has subsequently been suggested, was in fact some form of psychosomatic illness.[1] Tales of Cromwell's possibly hypochondriac tendencies, which nowadays we might prefer to explain as a depressive temperament, stretch back to his younger days: he is assumed to have consulted the eminent doctor Théodore de Mayerne in 1628 for *melancholia* – depression – though Mayerne's medical diagnosis may actually have been for a physical ailment, brought on by an excess of black bile (the literal meaning of *melan-cholē*), following the medical consensus about the importance of the four humours. What is more, we may in this case have the wrong 'Monsieur Cromwell', as Mayerne refers to him, who could equally have been his cousin Henry.[2] Similarly, the 'imposthume' was clearly a physical complaint, an abscess, rather than a mental illness, still less an imaginary one.[3] Cromwell himself plainly told Fairfax that he had suffered a 'dangerous sickness ... I received in myself the sentence of death, that I might learn to trust in Him that raises from the dead, and have no confidence in the flesh.'[4] If Cromwell's illness had a psychological element, it seems to have resided in the fact that recovering from it further reanimated his faith. What didn't kill him made him stronger.

Cromwell's correspondence with Fairfax is our best guide to his part in the next looming national crisis, though as always we must allow that it tells his side of the story. Parliament failed to deal with the New Model Army as fairly as they had done with the Scots. (In the event they didn't deal especially fairly with the Scots – they never paid the full amount promised – but they had, in the first instance, shown more willing.) Soldiers who were owed substantial arrears were expected to disarm and return home on the vaguest promises. The plan debated in the Commons in March 1647 to refashion part of the army as a force to quash the ongoing Irish rebellion was equally half formed, while suggested measures to remove all officers from England, except for the Lord General, Sir Thomas Fairfax, and later to insist that officers for the Irish force renew their commitment to the Covenant were all highly provocative. For, despite its sterling service in winning the war, the army had become doubly distasteful to the Presbyterian majority in Parliament: first, for its undoubted preference for Independent rather than Presbyterian religious government, and secondly because of a growing core of politically radical soldiers, and the emergence of a form of political organization to voice their agenda.

Such men, whom it seems that Cromwell first christened as 'Levellers' – those who wished to 'level' social distinctions based on wealth and property – included the consistently antagonistic John Lilburne. Having fallen foul of the House of Lords, Lilburne was in prison, where he remained from July 1646 until November the following year. But he was not to be silenced, writing to Cromwell in March 1647 accusing him of obstructing the soldiers' plans to petition Parliament and becoming steadily convinced that Cromwell meant to betray his old comrades as their aims diverged. But to begin with, the army's actual position was far less radical than the likes of Lilburne might have wished. The Petition that the army drew up and presented to Parliament at the end of March was a reasoned document issuing from both officers and the ranks requesting such unobjectionable measures as parliamentary indemnity for past actions, reliable prospects of settlement of arrears, regular pay for those who remained under arms, and provision for the disabled, widows and orphans.

In Parliament Denzil Holles led the over-reaction, perhaps fearing the signs of creeping democracy and a Leveller takeover, as evidenced by the new groups of army 'agitators' who contributed to the Petition. In truth, most of their radical contributions had been removed by army officers before the Petition was presented. In front of a thin House, Holles gathered enough support to pass what became known as the 'Declaration of Dislike'. It included a description of petitioning soldiers – those men who had finally delivered the king into Parliament's hands after four years of fighting and more than a decade of opposition and impasse – as 'enemies of the state'.

Unsurprisingly to all but Holles, the army did not respond positively to this latest insult. In part, their answer was personal. At a gathering of officers at the Essex town of Saffron Walden on 15 April, it became clear that only with their old commanders would they even contemplate service in Ireland: 'Fairfax and Cromwell, and we all go!'[5] Cromwell wasn't with the army at this point, but after the officers re-presented essentially the same petition to Parliament as had spawned the Declaration of Dislike, he was despatched at the beginning of May to Essex, along with fellow parliamentary veterans Henry Ireton (now his son-in-law), Charles Fleetwood and Philip Skippon, to negotiate a compromise.

Although Cromwell didn't appear to realize, it was too late for that. He and his fellow officer-negotiators clearly sympathized with their comrades, but their mistake was to believe that they could bring the Presbyterian majority in the House of Commons to a similar understanding. After three days, the four parliamentary commissioners sent a report to Westminster in which they backed the army's case, as having 'good ground'.[6] Cromwell had put to the officers what he took to be the gradual thawing of Parliament, including their offer of indemnity and a fortnight's pay. He seems to have believed that the majority in the army could be persuaded to disband, and to 'maintain a good opinion of that authority that is over both us [the officers] and them [the men]'. Certainly, that is what he reported to Parliament on his return, with only a few provisos.[7] But MPs ignored the concessions Cromwell had suggested, and proceeded with plans for disbandment, only to find that when they tried to put them into practice, the army had already decamped, with plans to muster in defiance of parliamentary orders near Newmarket.

Cromwell's part in this was seen by some at the time and by many since as characteristically scheming and Machiavellian, playing off a Parliament in which he had little support against an army which lacked political legitimacy but would follow him anywhere. As has often been pointed out, however, even had he wanted to, there was no need for Cromwell to act as the army's provocateur, leading them into a dispute with Parliament: the animosity of Holles and co. was provocation enough. As for the army, its officers and men needed no outside encouragement to believe what was true: Parliament wished to be rid of them, and wouldn't, or couldn't pay enough to do so. There was more to their dispute than money, as the 'agitators' in the army had begun to make clear: political reform and religious freedom were also on their agenda. But it seems likely that, as with the Scots, many less radically inclined officers and men would have been willing to stand down if they had been offered a proper incentive to do so. In words and deed, Parliament appeared to some to be treating its army with contempt.

For an understanding of Cromwell, this episode has two salient points. The first is that Cromwell himself did not play the key role. He had been sick, dismayed by the breakdown in relations between Parliament and the army, and while hardly inactive had not been the most conspicuous presence in negotiations after the end of hostilities. To the army, Fairfax, who had stayed with them despite his reservations (apart from a brief period when he suffered his own bout of illness), was a more significant figure at the time, while even among the parliamentary commissioners at Saffron Walden, Skippon was given equal weight with Cromwell. The second point is that Cromwell's own actions and words give no indication of duplicity. He may have been guilty of naïvely trusting that he could negotiate a solution – in other words of wishful thinking – a defect from which, for all the great power that eventually attached to him, he continued to suffer. But, as some modern commentators have observed, the split between Parliament and the army shows Cromwell in a familiar, and flawed, role of would-be coalition builder.[8] The trouble with coalitions, especially when they don't work, is that they satisfy nobody. Cromwell, accordingly, came under attack from all sides: Presbyterians, Royalists and army Levellers.

The fact that Cromwell chose this time to push for his own financial settlement, receiving almost £2,000 from Parliament for his arrears, was fuel for his critics. John Lilburne, still imprisoned in the Tower on parliamentary orders, seized on it: 'Accursed be the day that ever the House of Commons bribed you with a vote of 2,500*l* to betray and destroy us.'[9] But Lilburne saw conspiracies everywhere, which was understandable in a man who had suffered as much persecution as he had: before the Civil War he had been whipped, pilloried and imprisoned; during it he had clashed with superior officers, which had led to his current incarceration. Cromwell's payment was not conditional on his support for disbandment, and he is likely to have agreed with his fellow commissioner Skippon's verdict, in a letter to the Speaker of the Commons, that 'the disobliging of so faithful an army will be repented of'.[10]

For months, between his recovery in March and the final break between Parliament and army in late May 1647, Cromwell had been trying to bring the two sides together (while their vanquished enemy, the king, used his opponents' internal squabbles to play for time in his own negotiations). But now the moment was coming when he would have to choose between the two. The Cromwells had moved into a house in Drury Lane in London, and it was there that, on 31 May, he was visited by a junior New Model Army officer, Cornet George Joyce. What Cromwell and Joyce discussed is not known, but two days later Joyce arrived at Holmby House at the head of a troop of 500 horse, and removed the king from his parliamentary guard under Major-General Browne, whose garrison was loyal to the Presbyterian majority in Parliament, before setting off with him to Newmarket.

It seems unlikely, to say the least, that this momentous plan had not been mentioned at the meeting between Joyce and his far superior officer. Whether Joyce revealed his whole scheme, whether he told Cromwell that he planned merely to substitute his troops, loyal to the New Model Army, for Parliament's, and what Cromwell made of the plan, have all been the subject of speculation ever since. Those who could not believe that an officer as junior as Joyce would not be under orders have argued that Cromwell must have put him up to it. Indeed, perhaps the first to do so was Charles I: 'he [Joyce] could not venture to attempt such a thing as to bring me away, for it was Treason, but that he had the countenance of greater Persons', as the king told Fairfax, Cromwell and others at their first meeting.

But Joyce reminded him then that he had explicitly not claimed the generals' authority for his action, and the king conceded 'That it was true indeed, he did say so.'[11] If all this was put on for show, it was convincingly played. And men with even less authority in the army had begun in that spring of 1647 to voice their own opinions and formulate their own plans. Joyce did not necessarily need Cromwell to tell him what to do.

Whether the architect of the scheme or, more likely, a partially informed and interested party, Cromwell realized quickly that he could not keep up his balancing act any longer. Faced with threats of impeachment by a Parliament where the majority believed he had gone behind their backs and greatly exceeded his authority, and now with no prospect of effecting a negotiated solution between his two masters, he chose the army. The choice was not entirely motivated by the wish to avoid imprisonment. In the army, Cromwell had surrounded himself with like-minded individuals and seen what godly men, the 'well affected', could accomplish in war. He had hoped to secure liberty for these men's 'tender consciences' in the peace that followed, but had been unable even to secure their back pay. When he failed to do so, the army had taken the most important bargaining chip of all into their own hands: the king. The choice to join them, and their Lord General Fairfax – who had himself been completely wrong-footed by the abduction of Charles – was not difficult. In his memoirs, the Royalist officer John Berkeley, who was later sent to negotiate with Cromwell and Ireton, characterized the Levellers' view of Cromwell as the eternal trimmer, ready always to speak untruth for power, but the point Berkeley made that 'when he quitted the Parliament, his chief dependence was on the army, which he endeavoured by all means to keep in unity' is difficult to argue against.[12]

If Cromwell had had an elaborate plan to use Charles and the army to make himself more powerful, the events of the next few months showed that neither party was biddable. With Charles in their hands, the army now took the business of negotiating a settlement with him on themselves. The position they set out was designed to answer their own requirements as well as impose a lasting solution to Charles's position. Parliament was not excluded from the envisaged outcome, though Independent MPs, rather than Presbyterians, now came to the fore in negotiating it. But these new arrangements proved to be no more successful at answering the various problems thrown up by the Civil War than previous ones. Charles continued to resist agreement after the army drew up new negotiation terms, known as the Heads of the Proposals, in July 1647. Cromwell's son-in-law Henry Ireton is traditionally credited with formulating these terms – perhaps the most generous ever offered to the king – though recently it has also been argued that Independents in Parliament, as well as the Council of Officers, had an input.[13] The Heads set out the army's vision for a post-war England and Wales. Parliament was to be biennial and would control the army and navy, while the king would retain executive power along with a Council of State elected by Parliament. There was to be no established Church, but no imposition of Presbyterianism: Cromwell's liberty of conscience was on the menu. There would be indemnity for Parliamentarians, but earlier plans to punish long lists of Royalists were now much reduced.

From a mixture of stubbornness, lack of trust that what was offered could be delivered, and covert plans to return to war, Charles could not be persuaded to agree. Many of the army's problems remained internal, though it would intervene effectively to exclude the Presbyterian element from Parliament and turn back an armed attempt by the City governors to seize power and impose their own settlement. There was increasing noise from those who wished for a more radical constitutional solution than had been put forward in the Heads of the Proposals. The document in which this was enshrined, *An Agreement of the People*, was published in October, after negotiations with the king had been going on for three months without progress. The *Agreement* proposed to wipe the constitutional slate clean, reforming Parliament, gesturing towards manhood suffrage, allowing freedom of religion, and not even mentioning the office of king or House of Lords. Cromwell had negotiated face to face with Charles in the summer in his combined role as MP and army grandee, and then with the disaffected in the army in the autumn. It is difficult to say which he found harder. Certainly, neither negotiation yielded anything concrete, although at Putney, where Fairfax quartered the army to keep watch on the City, some principles emerged that would last much longer than Charles's reliance on his own indispensability.

Cromwell's role in what have come to be known as the Putney debates, during which the radical proposals of the *Agreement of the People* were scrutinized by senior officers and men, was his by now familiar one of compromiser: trying to hold the centre ground in the face of more extreme proposals. Putney is still remembered today as the place where the idea of 'one man one vote' was first aired, not least because the case for it was expressed in such memorable terms by Colonel Thomas Rainsborough, addressing Henry Ireton, in one of those moments when a voice seems to emerge from history and speak directly to us: 'really I think that the poorest he that is in England hath a life to live, as the greatest he; and therefore truly, sir, I think it's clear, that every man that is to live under a government ought first by his own consent to put himself under that government; and I do think that the poorest man in England is not at all bound in a strict sense to that government that he hath not had a voice to put himself under . . .'[14] Ever since, in opposing Rainsborough's proposal for universal male suffrage, Cromwell and Ireton seem to have been on the wrong side of an argument that resonates far beyond the squabbling over forms of worship or government, or even about the fate of Charles I. But in truth, Rainsborough's remarks, made at a prayer meeting before a session of the debate rather than at the debate itself, do not seem to have become the lasting focus of many at the time – even of those Levellers who might have been expected to have been sympathetic to them.

For both sides, there were other priorities. For Cromwell, Ireton and the army leadership, maintaining army unity in the face of a hostile body of Presbyterian opinion and the machinations of the king was paramount. On the army's side, those agitators who pressed for radical reform seemed far more interested in the settlement of the soldiers' own position, the protection of liberty of conscience, reform of Parliament and the law, than with a wholesale, principled extension of the franchise.

The real sticking point for the army at Putney and beyond turned out to be what to do with the king, how far to go in removing him from power and punishing him for having led the country into civil war. Levellers who did discuss the vote were often happy to accept continued restrictions on it, not only confining it to men (even Rainsborough had not countenanced votes for women) but to those who were not servants or receiving alms, not exactly the 'poorest he'. To today's way of thinking, the vote is such a fundamental political right that it can be difficult to accept that, in the seventeenth century, those who advocated manhood suffrage were a small minority; and that those who disputed it, like Cromwell, were not reactionary betrayers of a popular revolutionary ideal, but adherents to the mainstream. Nevertheless, when Cromwell and his fellow generals acted to put down a mutiny at Ware in Hertfordshire in November, they presented themselves as preservers of army unity rather than the constitutional status quo. They did so successfully. Only one of the three army rendezvous that took place at that time showed mutinous tendencies, and the harsh discipline meted out – including the execution of one soldier – swiftly halted the spread of army dissent.

During their discussions about the fate of the king,

Cromwell was at pains to warn the company at Putney not to mistake their desire for retribution for the clear word of God on the matter. Like many present, Cromwell conceded that 'we all apprehend danger from the power of the King and from the Lords'. But he resisted the logic that said that Charles must therefore be removed. As he put it, he wasn't sure that in working to preserve the king on his throne, under whatever conditions, 'it is Babylon that we are going about to heal'.[15] To a modern observer, such conscientious wrestlings might look like window-dressing. But some godly men still viewed the office of king, if not the king himself, as divinely ordained. Attacking it was a matter not just of politics, but of conscience. On 11 November, however, Charles himself changed the terms of the debate, when he escaped from his captors at Hampton Court and made for the Isle of Wight.

Charles's escape played so neatly into Cromwell's hands that it has often been suggested (without any more than circumstantial evidence) that he was complicit in it. Charles had apparently hoped to find an ally in the Governor of the Isle of Wight, the disaffected parliamentary officer Robert Hammond. But Hammond, who also happened to be Cromwell's second cousin, was not to be turned, and instead incarcerated the king in Carisbrooke Castle. There, on 26 December 1647, Charles still managed to complete a secret agreement, the Engagement, with a faction of Scots, subsequently known as the Engagers, who agreed to invade England on his behalf in return for the imposition of Presbyterianism in England. In February the following year, a rebellion began in south-west Wales against the

New Model Army and the Engagement became public knowledge. Such a dramatic demonstration of the king's untrustworthiness may have provided Cromwell with the sign he sought. Even if we can't be sure that these events made up Cromwell's mind to support the idea of trying Charles for his crimes, they did for others in the army. In April 1648, at a prayer meeting in Windsor Castle that Cromwell probably did not attend, officers agreed that, if they won the war that was now about to start, they would 'call Charles Stuart, that man of blood, to account'.[16]

Before that could happen, and whatever form the calling to account would take, Parliament needed to win a war. Although still under the command of Fairfax, who had inherited his father's barony in March, Cromwell was nevertheless emerging as the New Model Army's undisputed champion, even if he encountered some obstacles. Charles's decision to reopen hostilities through the Engagers, despite still being in captivity, encouraged Royalist uprisings in the south-east and Wales as well as the north, in anticipation of a Scottish invasion. Cromwell, taking the fight westwards towards Wales, had initial successes at Chepstow and Tenby, but was then held up by a six-week-long siege of Pembroke Castle. After Pembroke's surrender Cromwell returned to England and, while Fairfax carried on a bitter, drawn-out siege of Colchester, he marched to Preston to confront a Scottish army led by the Duke of Hamilton. Hamilton had joined with an English Royalist force under Sir Marmaduke Langdale, while Cromwell combined his force with that of John Lambert. This was Cromwell's first battle as sole commander. The result was a vindication of the professionalism of the New Model Army, which triumphed spectacularly against a disunited and poorly led enemy, and of its decisive leader in the field. The battle was hard fought over three days, with Langdale's troops in particular putting up stiff resistance. Hamilton's infantry retreated but was pursued beyond Wigan, and he surrendered at Stafford. About 10,000 prisoners were taken, and perhaps 2,500 men were killed. On Parliament's side, losses were as little as 100.

In his letter to Parliament after the Battle of Preston, Cromwell estimated that their forces had been outnumbered by 21,000 to 8,600. Other estimates put the Scottish combined force at nearer 15,000 and Parliament's at 14,000. The numbers are significant in part because of the rhetorical use to which Cromwell put them. In the victory of (on his view) a vastly outnumbered force, Cromwell saw – predictably enough – 'nothing but the hand of God' and, in his letter to the Speaker of the House, made the ominous statement that 'they that are implacable and will not leave troubling the Land may speedily be destroyed out of the Land'.[17] The implications for Charles seem clear, but it is possible that Cromwell had actually not yet made up his mind, either about the king's person or a future government for the country, and may merely have been referring to the Scots invaders. In the circumstances, it may have suited him that there was still military work to be done: work that took him first to Scotland, in pursuit of the remainder of the Engagers' army, and to Edinburgh, where he concluded an agreement with the Marquess of Argyll, leader of Scottish Presbyterians who had successfully opposed the Engagers, before returning to a mopping-up operation in the north of England. At Pontefract, where Thomas Rainsborough had been killed while conducting the siege, Cromwell took command.

Cromwell stayed long at Pontefract, presiding over a siege that others could perfectly well have overseen – and did, after Cromwell left. If he knew what was about to unfold in the capital, he seems to have wanted to avoid it. In the south, after Colchester had fallen, the political situation had briefly returned to its previous pattern, in which Parliament – despite an earlier resolution not to do so – continued fruitless negotiations with the king, still imprisoned at Carisbrooke; while the army again demanded better treatment. Another formal demand, the Remonstrance of the Army – drafted by Henry Ireton after talks between Independents and Levellers at a pub near the Guildhall – was presented to the Commons on 18 November. It included unequivocal plans to try the king for his life, pressing for 'capital punishment upon the principal author and some prime instruments of our late wars'. The response of the Commons was first to ignore the Remonstrance while they considered what the king had offered – which was actually rather more than had been required of him by the Heads of the Proposals – and then to reject the Remonstrance on 1 December.

As far as the army was concerned, the Presbyterian element in Parliament's persistence with attempted negotiations with the king, despite his demonstrations of untrustworthiness and their earlier assurances that they would *not* negotiate, was proof that they no longer represented the will of the people. Five days later, several New Model

Army regiments surrounded Parliament, and Colonel Thomas Pride, who had fought with Cromwell at Preston, stood on the steps with a list of members to be arrested. Forty-five MPs were taken into custody, and a total of around 200 were kept out, or stayed out of the House, including those who had voted against the Remonstrance. Those that remained, who came to be known as the Rump, could be relied upon to give the army what it wanted.

Cromwell, ordered south by Fairfax over a week before, arrived in London hours after Pride's Purge had taken place. He claimed not to have known it was going to happen – which may have been true of the detail, if not the general outline, of the army's plans. But he did not try to distance himself any further from it: 'since it was done, he was glad of it, and would endeavour to maintain it'.[18] He knew what the implications were. That November, in two letters to his cousin Robert Hammond, then the king's gaoler, he had wrestled with the propriety of putting the king on trial, and overriding the will of Parliament to do so if necessary. Although Cromwell had run out of patience with Charles – 'this man, against whom the Lord hath witnessed' – he stopped short, unlike his son-in-law Henry Ireton, of the conclusion that this must mean the king's trial and death.[19]

He continued to look for a different solution to the problem, including offering the king a chance to stay on the throne as little more than a figurehead, or to abdicate, both of which Charles rejected. Cromwell may have expected Charles to do so, but this does not mean that the offer was purely cosmetic: plenty of his comrades had no such qualms. After the Restoration, Cromwell was consistently portrayed as having been bent on the king's destruction. The truth seems on the contrary to have been that he felt compelled to accept that it was the right thing, the godly thing, to do, but he carried on trying not to do it long after many of his allies had made up their minds. Though often seen as the embodiment of religiously inspired certitude, Cromwell actually seems to have been a champion ditherer. One explanation of the long delay in Pontefract is that Cromwell was characteristically staying out of a fraught political situation until the difficult decisions had been taken by others. He certainly had a knack of absenting himself at crucial moments, and his enemies may have been right to see his hand behind such episodes as Joyce's arrest of Charles I, the king's escape to the Isle of Wight (under the governorship of his cousin) or Pride's Purge, with all of which he can be associated. But through innocence or cunning, he left no fingerprints.

The distance between what Oliver Cromwell wrote and did is not so great that we can clearly catch him in a lie. So our understanding of his motivations has to fall back on our instincts about his sincerity. Plenty of contemporaries, from Royalists to Levellers, doubted it. But it seems most likely that Cromwell's absences stemmed from hesitancy rather than subterfuge. First, staying away didn't exonerate him in his opponents' eyes in any case, as he must have realized. It was his own conscience with which he was wrestling, not others' opinions. Secondly, he had shown before, on the battlefield and off it, a willingness to thrust himself into danger, to risk his reputation as well as his life. Episodes of low cunning are harder to identify. In the years to come, of regicide, Commonwealth and Protectorate, he would risk unpopularity or losing support if he believed that he was acting as God wanted him to. It was when he wasn't sure what Providence had planned for him that Oliver's disappearing act was also reprised.

At the climactic drama of the age, 'this last tragical expedition' as Clarendon, the Royalist historian who became Charles II's Lord Chancellor, called it – the trial of Charles I – Cromwell was very definitely present. Clarendon tells the story that Lady Fairfax, whose husband stayed away from the trial, made several interruptions from the gallery, and questioned the court's standing as unrepresentative of the will of the people. Another account says that she declared: 'Oliver Cromwell is a rogue and a traitor.'[20] Justice John Bradshaw, a judge of impeccably radical credentials, had been appointed Lord President of the court to try Charles. But now that the army, through a Commons it controlled, was directing events, and its commanding officer, Lord Fairfax, had absented himself at the crucial moment, Cromwell was widely understood to be the driving force behind the new politics. He attended all four days of the trial as one of the commissioners of the court, and according to one regicide who later tried to exonerate himself, Cromwell gave anyone who objected short shrift, snapping that 'it is not fit that the Court should be hindered from their duty by one peevish man'.[21]

When the sentence was passed, Cromwell's was the third of the fifty-nine signatures on the death warrant, after Bradshaw and Thomas Grey (Lord Grey of Groby, who had stood by Colonel Pride, pointing out those to be arrested during the purge). Many stories were told afterwards about Cromwell and the death warrant, which many even in the purged Parliament were reluctant to sign. One has Cromwell and the republican MP Henry Marten flicking ink at each other over the parchment like naughty schoolboys, as if they thought this gravest of historical moments was a lark. Another has one of the signatories, Richard Ingoldsby, physically restrained by Cromwell, his hand forced to write his name. Though Ingoldsby was the only regicide who secured a pardon after the Restoration, neither tale sounds particularly credible, and the evidence of the warrant itself, in the Parliamentary Archives, shows that if Ingoldsby's signature was forced, then between them he and Cromwell still managed some extremely elegant and confident flourishes.[22] Cromwell does not seem to have attended the execution itself. The legend of his cloaked figure being spied over the body the night afterwards, murmuring 'Cruel necessity', is one more colourful addition impossible to verify. But Cromwell had certainly come to believe that there was no choice in the matter.

With the beheading of Charles on 30 January 1649, England made its great constitutional leap in the dark. Kings had been deposed and killed before, as Bradshaw, passing sentence on Charles, reminded him. But that had always been to put another on the throne. Those who had executed Charles I had put an end not just to a king, but to kingship itself, formalized by a vote in Parliament for its abolition in the first week of February. (The acts for 'abolishing the kingly office', and the House of Lords, were not actually passed until late March.) But who had executed Charles? That is, beyond the names on the death warrant, who supported the new direction? The question that the king himself (and Lady Fairfax) had raised about the authority of the court applied to the whole government of the nation. If ever Parliament could have been said to represent the general will, it did not do so now. Even its Rump, as the remainder of the Long Parliament came to be known, was not entirely convinced of the new dispensation, and an election along any lines would surely have returned a majority which opposed the execution of the king. The fact was that an extreme wing of the army, of which Cromwell was now the leading representative, had taken control. Cromwell had been one of the most popular parliamentary leaders, but his identification with a narrow strand of army republicans shrank that popularity, in spite of the victories to come. Attempts to broaden the basis of their government exercised Cromwell for most of the rest of his life, when he was not on campaign – and sometimes even then.

Despite his growing power, Cromwell was still not the sole director of policy in what became known as the Commonwealth. He was an MP in the Rump Parliament, which expanded periodically from its low point after Pride's Purge, but which still averaged around only fifty members at any vote at which they were counted throughout its four-year existence.[23] The new executive body, on which Cromwell sat, was the Council of State, but he was one of only two officers to be appointed, so that the Rump managed to replicate the old division between Parliament and the army without actually being independent of the latter. The constitution under which they would govern was not settled for five months. A revised *Agreement of the People*, with Leveller input, had been submitted before the king's trial, but its approval became bogged down amid accusations of treachery by Lilburne and his fellow Levellers. Lilburne claimed to have eavesdropped on Cromwell banging his fist on the table in the Council of State and shouting that 'you have no other way to deal with these men but to break them or they will break you; yea and bring all the guilt of blood and treasure shed and spent in this kingdom upon your heads and shoulders'. The Levellers and their supporters were, Cromwell raged, 'a despicable, contemptible generation of men'.[24]

The split between Cromwell and the Levellers – with many of whom, like Lilburne, he had served in arms – was sealed at Burford in Oxfordshire, where he confronted a Leveller army mutiny that broke out in May 1649. Both Fairfax, still Lord General of the Army, and Cromwell approached the threat presented by the Levellers to army unity in much the same way as they had the previous defiance at Ware in 1647. They tried to reassure those who could be drawn back with promises of support, but made examples of the ringleaders. At Burford, after Cromwell arrested and imprisoned 340 mutineers in the church, there were five courts martial. Three soldiers were executed by firing squad outside the church. Although Lilburne and other Leveller pamphleteers would con-tinue to voice their disdain for 'England's new chains' whenever they found the opportunity, the radical political possibilities of the Commonwealth were being closed off in an attempt to find a governing solution that could take more of the country – or at least more of the establishment – with it. Cromwell's own sentiments are perhaps not best dismissed in Lilburne's version of his former comrade's words, in that he continued to believe in much of what the Levellers had espoused, especially in terms of freedom of religion. In terms of his political reputation, however, Burford was the place where Oliver Cromwell lost the Left, those eventual inheritors of what came to be enshrined as the 'Good Old Cause', the socialist and labour movements. An annual Levellers Day at the village, otherwise the epitome of Cotswolds prosperity, still commemorates the soldiers' defiance of Cromwell's 'dictatorship'.[25]

If there was a dictatorship in England in 1649, it was not Cromwell's alone. He was still second in command of the army, even if Fairfax's influence (as a marginalized Presbyterian) and appetite (having avoided the trial of the king) were clearly waning. And he was still beholden to a Parliament which had yet to settle on its own principles of government. On 19 May 1649, two days after the executions in the churchyard at Burford, the Rump eventually passed its act declaring England to be a Commonwealth, 'governed by the Representatives of the People in Parliament, and by such as they shall appoint and constitute as Officers and Ministers under them for the good of the People, and that without any King or House of Lords'. It was a piece of legislation that left almost everything to the imagination about how such a revolutionary experiment was to be conducted, and in particular – since

the Leveller proposal for annual parliaments and a broad-
ened franchise had been so comprehensively rejected – how
the 'representatives of the people' were to be selected.

The spark for the mutiny in the army had not been the
work of the Levellers alone, but was again the soldiers'
reaction to the prospect of being sent against their will to
Ireland – which the Levellers co-opted for their case. With
haunting foresight, in view of the reputation that Cromwell's eventual Irish campaign gained, a Leveller pamphlet,
The English Soldier's Standard, warned of taking the fight
to Ireland, 'It will be no satisfaction to God's justice to
plead that you murdered men in obedience to your general.' It was not just that the army's men were tired of
fighting: some saw an Irish campaign as morally flawed
from the beginning, especially while 'those rights and lib-
erties of the people, for which you took up arms in
judgment and conscience', had not yet been secured.[26] The
proposed leader of the Parliamentarian force to go to Ireland was, unsurprisingly, Oliver Cromwell. Though the
expedition had been mooted at the beginning of the year,
Cromwell held out until he could be sure that it would
be properly financed and his own authority would be
unquestioned, before accepting his appointment as Lord
Lieutenant.

His task was to put an end to the Catholic rebellion that
had been continuing in one way or another since before the
outbreak of the other kingdoms' civil wars. This uprising
now showed signs of taking on a new lease of life from
Royalist input following the proclamation of Charles's son
as Charles II in February 1649, and the likelihood that any

attempt to re-establish the monarchy would be launched from Ireland or Scotland. Scotland initially looked less favourable, as the Scots continued to insist that the new king agree to impose the Presbyterian Covenant, which Charles resisted at first. In Ireland, there were fewer obstacles for a Royalist revival. The Stuarts' viceroy in Ireland, the Marquess of Ormond, had managed to negotiate a treaty with the Catholic Confederate rebels, who represented about two-thirds of Irish Catholics, weeks before Charles I's execution (a substantial force of Irish Catholics, under Owen Roe O'Neill, opposed the Confederation and remained outside the alliance). Cromwell himself had been a passionate advocate of the suppression of the rebellion since its outbreak in 1641, and had made several investments, as an Irish 'adventurer', in a parliamentary scheme to finance the Irish war in return for parcels of conquered rebel lands, which had, of course, not yet been 'recovered'. But his financial investment, on such risky terms, is perhaps better understood as a statement of faith: of a conviction that God would be revenged on Catholic rebels whose slaughter of English Protestants had been widely broadcast. Though Cromwell established the terms of his appointment with the dispassion of a professional soldier, he arrived in Ireland as an instrument of divine judgement.

Cromwell's Irish campaign became the most notorious blot on his reputation. As a strategic intervention his expedition, from his arrival on 15 August 1649 to his departure on 26 May the following year, was decisive, even if the rebellion did not formally end until April 1653, long after he had left. He was helped by the fact that, by the time he arrived in Ireland, his chief opponent Ormond had already been defeated at the Battle of Rathmines outside Dublin. Cromwell marched his 12,000 troops up the east coast northwards to Drogheda, and when the English Royalist commander, the one-legged Catholic Sir Arthur Aston, refused his summons to surrender, he bombarded the city before assaulting it. There was a fierce fight, before the great advantage in numbers on Cromwell's side told. It was after this that Cromwell gave his order not to 'spare any that were in arms in the town'. Aston was apparently battered to death with his own wooden leg. Cromwell returned briefly to Dublin before setting out south to Wexford, where another 2,000 defenders, priests and some other non-combatants were killed, many in cold blood. As disease began to ravage Cromwell's army, he went on to Waterford, which managed to hold out against his siege, and then attacked Clonmel, which only surrendered after its defenders had slipped away. Clonmel was the last Irish action in which Cromwell engaged. He left in May 1650, never to return.

Only those who have a wholly negative view of Cromwell and see that opinion vindicated in Ireland approach the nine months he spent there with any relish. But we do not have to have elevated him into a Carlylean Hero to recoil. We can do our best, as we must, to put his actions there in context, to say that terrible things had already happened in Ireland and Cromwell merely elaborated on a theme, to point out that by the contemporary 'laws of war' he did little that was unconscionable. The war in England

and Wales had sometimes become pitiless, for example when Fairfax refused to allow the evacuation of women and children during the siege of Colchester in 1648. We can also admit that Cromwell's visceral hatred of the Catholic Irish was Puritan orthodoxy (Pym had wanted Catholics to wear distinguishing clothing, for example, while 150 Irish prisoners had been tied back to back and thrown to their deaths in the sea off Pembroke in 1644 on the orders of a parliamentary vice-admiral). We can make comparisons with the awful massacres of the Thirty Years War, only just ended on the continent, to show that Cromwell's Irish campaign was not unusually bloody by the standards of the time. Contemporaries did so too, comparing the events at Drogheda and Wexford to the slaughter at the siege of Magdeburg in 1631, in which as many as 20,000 died.[27]

But the difficulty with all this is that Cromwell himself has in other cases left us so many insights into the way his fanatical zeal could be tempered by a genuine humanity that when we see it given full rein, as it was in Ireland, it makes the task of historical empathy much harder. Cromwell felt keenly the horror of war, the evil of those who 'have imbrued their hands in so much innocent blood', as he described the Irish he faced at Drogheda, referring to the massacres widely reported in 1641. But there he took that widely shared opinion as a licence to interpret the conventions of siege warfare in the most uncompromising way, and had no sense that at Drogheda it was he who was imbruing his hands. Subsequently at Wexford, there was an even less justifiable slaughter as terms of surrender were being negotiated, though in that case it is likely that Cromwell's troops were out of control.

If there was a strategic justification in killing all those who refused a 'summons' of a town to surrender – *pour encourager les autres* – it was not one that had been applied so harshly in England. And Cromwell's characteristically messianic letters to Parliament and the Council of State after Drogheda, in which he encourages them to 'give the glory of this to God alone, to whom indeed the praise of this mercy belongs', show that, for all his concession that 'such actions . . . cannot but work remorse and regret', he suffered little genuine self-doubt on this occasion. It is hard to read the sentences 'I believe we put to the sword the whole number of the defendants', shortly followed by 'And I truly believe that this bitterness will save much effusion of blood', without concluding that their author was a stranger to irony.[28] Taking Cromwell on his own terms, moreover, does little to absolve him: as many as half of his 3,000-odd victims at Drogheda were not Catholics, and none had been among the Irish Confederate rebels responsible for the massacres of 1641, so they were hardly complicit. In fact, many were English, including their commander: the Irish folk memory of Cromwell as an English scourge passes over the fact that even in Ireland, many of his victims were his own countrymen.

By the time Cromwell left Ireland in May 1650, the campaign had cost almost all the men he had set out with, though he had received reinforcements and vast amounts of money. It was only really after Cromwell's death that the blight on his reputation can be added to the bill. And

it should be added that the use Parliament went on to make
of his conquest after 1652, turning it into a form of ethnic
cleansing under which all Catholic landowners were forced
to move to Connacht, leaving more than half Ireland's land
mass to Protestant English 'adventurers', was not his
responsibility, or not his alone. At the time, Parliament's
Lord Lieutenant appeared to have succeeded where so
many others had failed. If some in England had hoped that
Ireland would swallow up Cromwell's ambitions in military disaster, as it had for so many before him, they would
be disappointed. Those English radical voices that had
been raised against the morality of the Irish campaign
might have seen their fears confirmed, but, more broadly,
Cromwell's contemporary standing was only boosted by
his Irish campaign. One consequence of that success was
that Cromwell was the only realistic candidate to lead Parliament's military response to the next Royalist threat. In
June 1650, Charles II concluded a treaty with the Scots,
and shortly afterwards he arrived in the country to prepare
an invasion. Returning home from Ireland to a triumphant
welcome, Cromwell almost immediately put in a request to
Parliament to lead an army to Scotland.

He was to do so as that army's Lord General. Fairfax
was first asked to resume command, but he declined to
take the field against his fellow Presbyterians. The Scottish
campaign thus marked the occasion when Cromwell
accepted his promotion – with a reluctance that seemed
genuine to observers at the time, but was in hindsight
widely seen as 'acted' – to supreme command of the army,
a role which many believed he had already been occupying

for some months.[29] It was as 'General of the Forces of the Parliament of the Commonwealth of England' that he led a force in July of around 16,000 men into Scotland against David Leslie's Covenanters, who numbered as many as 20,000.

Though the threat of a Royalist alliance had been used to bring about the invasion, the army that Cromwell eventually faced at Dunbar on 3 September 1650 was not part of such an alliance. It was the armed wing of the Presbyterian Kirk, implacably opposed to England's parliamentary leaders who had triumphed over the Presbyterian element following Pride's Purge. Despite their differences, Cromwell tried to win over the Scots in one of his best-remembered phrases: 'I beseech you, in the bowels of Christ, think it possible you may be mistaken.'[30] At Dunbar, despite being outnumbered almost two to one, with a force reduced by disease to as little as 11,000, Cromwell achieved perhaps his most impressive victory. As before, it was a triumph of belief as much as of tactics, this time in a clash with an equally committed foe: 'The Enemy's word was, *The Covenant* . . . ours, *The Lord of Hosts*', and, as at Marston Moor, Cromwell's opponents were 'made by the Lord of Hosts as stubble to our swords'. It was reported that Cromwell had burst into laughter at the extent of the victory.[31]

As with earlier judgements of God on the battlefield, he also drew some practical lessons. Here was support for the political programme that he viewed as godly: 'relieve the oppressed, hear the groans of poor prisoners in England; be pleased to reform the abuses of all professions'.[32] The victory, in which as many as 3,000 Scots were killed and

1. Cromwell as Lord Protector, with the symbols of royalty. This engraving of his wooden and wax effigy was made in 1659, shortly after his death.

The Religious sucessfull and truly Vallian
Lieutenant Generall Cromwell

2a. 'The Religious Sucessfull and truly Valliant Lieutenant Generall Cromwell': one of the earliest known images, made in the 1640s.

2b. The Leveller John Lilburne, in a familiar setting, demonstrating 'The liberty of the Freeborne English-Man conferred on him by the House of Lords', 1646.

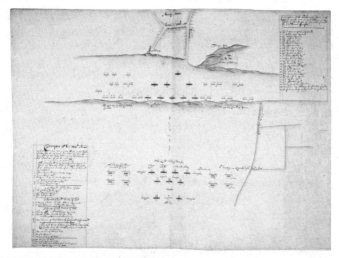

3. A contemporary battle plan of Naseby, 1645.

A

REMONSTRANCE

OF

Many Thousand Citizens, and other Free-born

PEOPLE OF ENGLAND,

To their owne House of

COMMONS.

Occasioned through the Illegall and Barbarous Imprisonment
of that Famous and Worthy Sufferer for his Countries
Freedome, Lievtenant Col.

JOHN LILBURNE.

Wherein their just Demands in behalfe of themselves and the whole
Kingdome, concerning their Publike Safety, Peace and Freedome, is
Exprest'd; calling those their Commissioners in Parliament to an Account, how they (since the beginning of their Session, to this present)
have discharged their Duties to the Universallity of the People, their
Soveraigne LORD, from whom their Power and Strength is derived, and by whom (ad bene placitum,) it is continued.

London

July 7th   Printed in the Yeer. 1646.

4a. Cromwell and Charles I by Paul Delaroche, 1831.
The German poet Heinrich Heine described Cromwell as
looking 'like a woodman who has just felled an oak'.

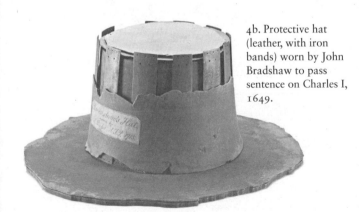

4b. Protective hat
(leather, with iron
bands) worn by John
Bradshaw to pass
sentence on Charles I,
1649.

THE
VVorld turn'd upside down:
OR,
A briefe description of the ridiculous Fashions
of these distracted Times.

By T.J. a well-willer to King, Parliament and Kingdom.

London : Printed for *John Smith.* 1647.

5. The Royalist view of the Civil War, 1647, by John Taylor.

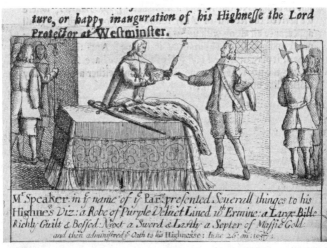

ture, or *happy inauguration of his Highnesse the Lord Protector at Westminster.*

Mr Speaker. in ye name of ye Parlt presented Severall thinges to his Highnes Viz: a Robe of Purple Veluet Lined wth Ermine: a Large Bible Richly Guilt & Bossed: Next a Sword & Lastly a Septer of Massie Gold. and then administred ye Oath to his Highnesse: Iune 26. an 1657.

6a. Cromwell's reinvestiture as Lord Protector, 1657. The ceremony was quasi-regal, from the Speaker's addressing Cromwell as 'Highness' to the 'Severall thinges' presented to him: purple robe lined with ermine, gold sceptre, as well as Bible and sword.

6b. Robert Walker's portrait of Cromwell as General, 1649, around the time of the Irish expedition.

7a. Cromwell's letter to the House of Commons after the victory at Naseby, in which he encouraged Parliament to promote liberty of conscience, 1645.

7b. A favourable answer to a petition of the East India Company, 1657, in which Protector Cromwell uses the royal 'we'.

8a. Cromwell's death mask, taken from his funeral effigy.

8b. Cromwell's burial plaque, removed from his coffin in 1661, showing the arms of the Protectorate, and its motto *Pax Quaeritur Bello* (peace is sought by war).

10,000 taken prisoner, and only twenty of Cromwell's men were lost (according to his own estimate), was welcomed not only by the English Parliament but also – clearly an unintended consequence – by the Royalists in Scotland, who correctly saw this as the death knell for the Covenant, and a chance to make a full alliance with Scottish Stuart sympathizers. In January 1651 the Marquess of Argyll, with whom Cromwell had previously collaborated, crowned Charles II king at Scone Abbey.

Cromwell's Scottish campaign lasted another six months: not because the new alliance posed a particularly formidable threat, but because the Lord General fell ill, first with the dysentery that had racked his army, then with kidney stones. He was fifty-one years old, had been on campaign off and on for almost a decade, and was feeling the strain. The day after Dunbar he wrote to Elizabeth, his 'beloved Wife': 'I have been in my inward man marvellously supported; though I assure thee, I grow an old man, and feel infirmities of age marvellously stealing upon me.' In April he was able to tell her that 'I am increased in strength in my outward man', but it was not until June that he was well enough to resume the fight.[33] In July 1651 he combined with his deputy, Major-General John Lambert, in drawing the Scots into battle again, and Lambert won another victory over them at Inverkeithing, just north of Edinburgh. Cromwell continued north, to Perth, cutting off the Scottish army's access to reinforcements, forcing them to march south and gamble everything on an invasion of England. They were chased and harassed by several Parliamentarian forces, which drove them westwards for three weeks, away from the road to London. They reached Worcester before a vastly bigger Parliamentarian army caught up with them. With the delay of a day – which might have been deliberate – Cromwell was able to face the Scots on the anniversary of Dunbar, and on 3 September 1651 he dealt what appeared to be the final blow to Royalist hopes. As far as Cromwell was concerned, this last victory, the final battle in which he participated, was indeed 'for aught I know, a crowning mercy'. Charles II got away, experiencing the picaresque adventures for which his personality seemed better suited than the grim business of war. Royalism was a lost cause. That much appeared to be confirmed not only by the defeat, but also by the signal lack of support or rallying to his colours that Charles's army experienced as it marched through England. For nearly a decade, while Cromwell lived, it remained so.

That, however, was not necessarily how Cromwell saw it. Even after Worcester, there were men both inside and outside the Rump Parliament who could still contemplate a monarchy, and a Stuart sitting on the throne. Remarkably, Cromwell seems to have been one of them. In his recollections of the events of the middle of the century published after the Restoration, a former supporter of Cromwell, Bulstrode Whitelocke, gave an account of a meeting convened by the Lord General in December 1651 between a group of senior MPs and senior officers to discuss the future constitution. From their conversation, it emerges that no one thought the Commonwealth's brief declaration of 1649 of a government 'without any King or House of Lords' had settled the matter. While most of the officers present at the discussion were in favour of a kingless republic, most of the MPs preferred to contemplate 'a mixt Monarchical Government . . . suitable to the Laws and People of this Nation, and if any Monarchical, I suppose we shall hold it most just to place that Power in one of the sons of the late King'. Though voices were heard in reply for a republic, the fact that thoughts quickly turned to which of Charles's sons would be most acceptable is an indication of how comfortable some of the assembled company appeared to be with the idea of restoring a king. When it was suggested that even Charles II might be widely accepted, the man who had just fought against him was sceptical: 'That will be a Business of more than ordinary difficulty,' Cromwell said, but he was not against the principle: 'really I think, if it may be done with safety, and preservation of our Rights, both as Englishmen, and as Christians, that a Settlement with somewhat of the Monarchical Power in it, would be very effectual'.[34]

For a man who had just fought two bloody campaigns on behalf of a kingless commonwealth, this was a remarkable statement. Whether Cromwell's equivocation about the ease of a Stuart restoration was a way of promoting his own candidature is difficult to say. Famously, Whitelocke recorded a later private conversation in which Cromwell disingenuously enquired, 'What if a man should take upon him to be King?', and received from Whitelocke a less than encouraging reply. The fact that no one at the earlier meeting – when barely two months had passed since Cromwell's latest demonstration of his providential value to his nation – had thought to enquire of the Lord General if he might consider taking up the burden of the crown himself, should perhaps have made him realize that the exceptional circumstances in which such an offer could be imagined had not yet arisen. But if he took any conclusion from the discussion, it can only have been that the English, or at least those classes of Englishmen whom he saw as suited for choosing governments, were not naturally inclined towards republicanism.

Over the next two years, Cromwell had a place as both an MP and a leading member of the Council of State, as well as his role as commander of the army, which placed him at the head of the Council of Officers. All these prominent roles could not, however, combine to bend Parliament to his will. In fairness to Cromwell, what can be discerned of his wishes at this time was not some personal agenda, but widely shared hopes for a dissolution of Parliament and plans for its reconstitution along lines that might 'heal' the divides of the Civil War; and religious reforms along Independent lines, allowing for liberty of conscience and the propagation of the Gospel. How widely shared is difficult to say, but these were certainly matters that exercised the army, and during these years Cromwell found himself in his habitual position of serving two masters, the army and Parliament. As before, he eventually came down on the side of those who had, as far as he was concerned, risked so much more in the cause of liberty.

Eventually Cromwell lost patience with the Rump, interrupting a bill-reading and dissolving Parliament by force in April 1653, in a scene matching in drama Charles I's intervention to arrest the five members (though Cromwell was, of course, a sitting MP, so he did at least have a right to be present, if not to do what he did). It is possible that the Rump may actually have been on the way to answering some of Cromwell's wishes. It was later claimed that the bill whose reading Cromwell so violently interrupted was one to establish a procedure for new elections, but we will never know for sure. As well as clearing the mace away ('What shall we do with this bauble? Here, take it away') and summarily dismissing his fellow MPs ('You are no Parliament ... I will put an end to your sitting'), Cromwell snatched up the bill under debate, and it has never been seen again.

If we can't know exactly why Cromwell acted against the Rump when he did, beyond an obvious loss of patience, it is possible to say from what came afterwards what his intentions were, even if they, too, might have been changed by events. To begin with, they were very clearly not to restore the monarchy or assume power himself, as that was not what he implemented – though both were popular topics of discussion. Some gossiped that 'he intends to call home the young king', while others apostrophized Cromwell himself in May as a 'great Captain and Prince' who would 'ascend three Thrones' (of England, Ireland and Scotland).[35] Instead, the reduced Council of State that was brought in days after the dismissal of the Rump as an executive body to carry on day-to-day business was not, as in so many cases of military takeovers, a permanent front for a dictatorship or oligarchy. The legislative body that was eventually put in place, however, though it too was planned as a temporary measure, was a unique creation in English history. Summoned in June and sitting from July 1653, it was an Assembly rather than a Parliament, made up of 140 members nominated by a majority vote of the army's Council of Officers rather than elected. They are generally (and rather misleadingly) known as 'Barebone's Parliament' (after one of their number, Praisegod Barebone, a lay preacher and Leathersellers Warden who was not as hot a Protestant as he sounds).

Cromwell is in part responsible for the caricature of this body as a group of religious extremists and social levellers. But socially and religiously, the Nominated Assembly was not unlike earlier parliamentary bodies. Whatever its virtues, however, only five months into a term that was scheduled to last for sixteen, it too were dissolved, after its own disagreements made progress impossible. This time the more conservative members voted their own dissolution and presented their decision to Cromwell as a fait accompli. Cromwell had had high hopes for the Assembly, outlined in a lachrymose two-hour speech at its opening. But he and his fellow officers had seen the failure of the Assembly coming, and Cromwell had nodded at Major-General Lambert's contingency plans, contained in a document called the Instrument of Government. Originally, the Instrument contained a proposal to confer the title of king on Oliver, but, perhaps remembering the discouraging words of Bulstrode Whitelocke, Cromwell refused to hear of it. So on 16 December 1653, at Westminster Hall, four days after the Nominated Assembly had offered up its resignation, Oliver Cromwell was invested in another title with a long history: Lord Protector.

5
Lord Protector

Oliver Cromwell's emergence as head of state would not have surprised opponents who had been warning of his ambitions since the 1640s, in pamphlets with titles such as *A Coffin for King Charles a Crowne for Cromwell*.[1] Supporters of the Parliament and Commonwealth might have expected it too. Though discussions about forms of government during the Commonwealth had not reached a consensus on the appeal of 'mixt monarchy', the continuing focus on Cromwell in print and image between 1649 and 1653 had done nothing to break the habit of concentrating the culture of government on an individual. When Cromwell had the parliamentary mace seized as he dismissed the Rump, he may not have intended it, but he was flinging out one of the rare examples of a newly commissioned piece of Commonwealth iconography. The parliamentary symbols on the Commonwealth mace had replaced the regal and dangerously 'popish' ones of crown and cross on its predecessor. More often, Cromwell was held up as his government's answer to royalty. In 1649, on the eve of his Irish expedition, he had allowed himself to be painted by Robert Walker as an idealized warrior in antique armour, with a courtly page tying his sash as he fixes his gaze on the viewer, a marshal's baton in his hand. Other Parliamentarians had been depicted in similar fashion, notably Sir Arthur Heselrige, whose martial portrait (sans page) in the same pose, it has recently been suggested, was painted over one of Oliver.[2] But the image Cromwell approved, and which was reproduced across the country in copies and engravings, shows him in posture and dress reminiscent of Anthony Van Dyck's portraits not only of the Earl of Strafford, his doomed Royalist predecessor as Lord Lieutenant, but even of Charles I and his offspring.

As Lord Protector, Cromwell would continue to employ painters who copied Van Dyck's opulent style, even if, in subtle ways, these images would also be distinguished from those of royal predecessors. Although he had resisted attempts to single him out on a medal to commemorate the victory at Dunbar, on his return from the Battle of Worcester he had allowed himself to be greeted just as a victorious monarch would have been, by the City corporation, who led him into London in a procession watched by thousands. Expanding from these pioneering gestures, between 1653 and Oliver's death in 1658 the Protectorate was able to establish a form of legitimacy and wide acceptance. It did so without (quite) becoming a monarchy, but increasingly by allowing Oliver to be portrayed as the equivalent of monarch: a man, if not anointed, then certainly chosen by God, fitted for rule less by popular acclamation than divine approbation.

The Lord Protector had plenty of practical concerns to occupy him and his government over these five years, and several significant achievements. What he couldn't do was to create a convincing permanent substitute for monarchy. His own son was unable to attract the same sort of backing as Oliver when he succeeded him. (How could he have done? Oliver had established himself as a result of his achievements, which meant as much to his opponents who feared crossing him as it did to his supporters: on its own, the Cromwell name had none of the pulling power of royalty.) A return to Commonwealth government subsequently quickly unravelled. A nation that had been content with, or at least tolerant of, a form of kingship in the Protectorate could not be persuaded to fall back in line with a kingless Commonwealth. In that sense, the lesson of the Cromwellian experiment was that monarchy continued to appeal to those subjects who had a say in their political destiny. If opinion polls are to be trusted, it still does.

The experience of the Protectorate, and what followed it, showed that England had not abandoned the comforts of monarchy. But Cromwell discovered that the struggles of the 1640s had left the scope of action for a 'supreme legislative authority', when it 'resided[d] in one person, and the people assembled in Parliament', frustratingly restricted for that one person.[3] An irony of the first Protectorate, which was set up under the Instrument of Government and lasted until Cromwell and the Council of State dismissed the Protectorate Parliament in January 1655, was that its head found Parliament as obstructive to his concept of good government as Charles I had done in his time. Under the terms of the Instrument, MPs were to be 'persons of known integrity, fearing God, and of good conversation'. They were not to have fought against

Parliament since 1641, or to be Roman Catholics. These terms, perhaps unsurprisingly, proved to be far too broad if the purpose was to create a legislative body that would carry on what Oliver saw as the task of the Protectorate Parliament: 'healing and settling', to 'put the top-stone to this work, and make the nation happy'.[4]

What he meant by this was perhaps deliberately vague, but in the months before the opening of Parliament, in the vigorous work of the Council of State, there were some indications. The Council made moves to enforce a harsh policy in Ireland, and a slightly less rigorous approach, complete with a plan for union, towards Scotland. In this period, reforms of the legal system and the beginnings of a religious settlement along Cromwell's favoured lines, which permitted a broad interpretation allowing Independents, Presbyterians and Baptists to coexist, were also set in motion. Finally, the origins of perhaps the most enduring, if least glamorous, of Protectorate reforms, of government finances and the taxation system, were initiated in this period. In all, between January and September 1655 the Protector and his Council passed eighty pieces of legislation. In its nearly five months' sitting, before Cromwell gave in once again to his exasperation with parliaments, the Protectorate Parliament passed none.

Cromwell and the Council's decision to dissolve the Protectorate Parliament stemmed from more than impatience at its lack of energy and preoccupation with constitutional arrangements. What MPs had seemed to be on the verge of enacting didn't appeal much either. One objectionable feature was attacks on 'heretics', which appeared to leave the way open for an expansion of religious intolerance, in direct opposition to the Protector's hopes for 'union and right understanding between godly people'.[5] Threats to the army were another. Cromwell saw the army as the guarantee of a balanced constitutional settlement, the only body that could stop Parliament from engrossing and perpetuating its own power. If it occurred to him that there were equally legitimate fears that the army could be used to inflate his own power, he did not see that as a problem. The army, he told MPs, 'determines his [the Protector's] power . . . for doing the good he ought'. Cromwell's opponents habitually saw such self-justification as rank hypocrisy. In hindsight, it is Cromwell's sincerity, or his naïvety, that seems more striking. Success in battle and his own elevation to political pre-eminence, what Cromwell took to be the mark of God's favour, had made him ever more certain of himself. Someone who is convinced he is right, as Cromwell increasingly became, as Charles I was almost from the beginning, can be far more damaging than a hypocrite.

The period between Protectorate Parliaments, lasting from January 1655 to September 1656, is associated with Cromwellianism at its most earnestly raw. In fact, the epitome of the regime's authoritarianism, the Rule of the Major-Generals, was not instituted until August 1655, and did not come to an end until January 1657. This attempt to govern the country along military lines, with twelve major-generals responsible for individual regions, was not a purely Cromwellian solution. During this period Cromwell worked closely with his Council, and John Lambert, the author of the Instrument of Government, was the driving force behind the establishment of the major-generals' regime. In October 1655, instructions were issued to these new satraps which give an impression of the Protectorate's ambitions and its sense of embattlement, surrounded by Royalist plots on the one hand, and the spread of 'ungodliness' on the other. There had indeed been a Royalist conspiracy, the little-supported and easily crushed Penruddock's rising in and around Salisbury in March 1655, but the Protector and his Council took the opportunity it presented to introduce a form of administration that was reminiscent of the military divisions of the country in the early 1640s. In effect, and despite the fact that all three former kingdoms were under the government's control, the Protectorate was acting as if the Civil War was still being fought.

Royalists and 'papists' were not the only groups whom the major-generals were directed to monitor – though only they were made to pay for the new set-up through a 'decimation tax', and only they were subject to a formal registration system and a requirement to take out bonds against good behaviour. The last government to have been forced to such an expedient was Richard III's, but he at least had the justification of a genuine threat to his regime. The other menace that Cromwell's appointees were to look out for was the one whose suppression has made his name synonymous to some with Puritan joylessness: the spectre of 'Prophaneness and Ungodliness'. This would be manifest in 'Drunkenness, Blaspheming, and taking of the Name of God in vain, by swearing and cursing, Plays and

Interludes, and prophaning the Lord's day'. In fact, there were already laws against these 'abominations' (and the notorious ordinance to abolish the feast of Christmas, along with Easter and Whitsun, had been passed in 1647). But the major-generals were sternly tasked with their 'more effectual execution'.[6]

To modern eyes, fears about the security of the regime – whether centred on Royalist threats or the failures in the 'Western Design' to capture Hispaniola from the Spanish – look like separate, 'political' concerns in contrast to the programme for the introduction of 'godly reformation'. But it should not surprise us that Cromwell, whose politics, military and personal financial decisions were so openly governed by a belief that they followed a Providential path, should feel compelled to enforce a similar outlook on the nation at large, when the Lord had seen fit to place it in his care – or that he should view the failures of foreign policy as a divine judgement on domestic conduct. From the time he had first taken up arms, as he had boldly explained to John Hampden, Cromwell equated the chances of success with encouraging those 'as had the fear of God before them'. The Instructions to the Major-Generals showed an intention to elaborate on the good work.

Lord Protector, Council and the major-generals themselves all seemed to have been convinced of the rightness and indeed the popularity of their cause. That is the best explanation for the major-generals' confidence, when the government was forced to review the regime's finances, in predicting that a new Parliament would support their work. In fact, when in 1656 new parliamentary elections were duly held, it became clear that there was widespread opposition to the regime. The Council, apparently without Cromwell's input, as he later claimed not to have agreed with their actions, were only able to ensure a quiescent Parliament by excluding as many as 100 MPs, while around sixty more reacted to the purge by not taking their seats. The Council was acting within the letter of the Instrument of Government in taking this action, but it only confirmed suspicions that they (and their master Cromwell) had no interest in free elections, or a truly independent Parliament. The remaining members seem to have been encouraged by the Protector's confidence that the 'liberty and prosperity of this nation depend upon reformation, to make it a shame to see men to be bold in sin and profaneness'.[7] Unlike the previous Parliament, this one went about its work with vigour, sending Cromwell seventy-one acts for his assent.

Even this Parliament, however, could not be relied on to stay united for long. Soon, the same fault lines that had fractured the first Protectorate Parliament, and indeed previous parliaments in various forms, began to re-emerge. Religious (in)tolerance and military funding and establishment were, once again, the sticking points. The issue of Parliament's authority over religious practice was highlighted by a colourful case in which a Quaker minister, James Nayler, committed what most took to be a 'horrid blasphemy' when he re-enacted Jesus's entry into Jerusalem on Palm Sunday, by riding a donkey into Bristol while Quaker women strewed palms before him. The condemnation of this rather literal imitation of Christ was almost universal, but a number of MPs, Council members and probably the Protector himself were troubled by the idea that Parliament would decide what constituted blasphemy and, potentially, threaten a transgressor with death.

The army's role in government resurfaced in a reintroduced Militia Bill, which had the unhappy effect of reopening discussions about how permanent to make measures against former Royalists. Under the terms of the bill, it was envisaged that even those who had long since repented of their Royalism (and who were therefore covered by the Act of Oblivion, which only exempted from its blanket amnesty those who continued their anti-Parliamentary activities after January 1648) would go on paying the decimation tax which funded their own oppression. It was into these newly divided circumstances that the Miles Sindercombe plot introduced an element of urgency and danger. The outcome was that a group of MPs and Council members (it has never been established exactly who, though the case for the involvement of Cromwell's Secretary of State, John Thurloe, in whipping up fears of invasion in the wake of the plot has been convincingly made) gathered to concoct a Remonstrance, which was introduced in Parliament by Sir Christopher Packe on 23 February 1657. This document saw the solution to the Protectorate's problems in a reformed constitution, with an upper house to be nominated by the Lord Protector who, for his part, was to take a new title: that of king.

Both in Parliament and in the army there were instant objections to, as well as instant support for, the new offer, which was shortly formalized as the Humble Petition and Advice. This new version of the Remonstrance made it clear that Cromwell was expected to accept all or nothing: that is, if he wanted the rest of the settlement, including the Other House and the power to name his successor, then it must be as King Oliver.

It was not until May, more than two months after it had been presented, that Cromwell finally rejected the Remonstrance – rejected, that is, the part that insisted on his becoming king. In an epic speech he set out his reasons, and Parliament responded by acceding to his wishes, going back on their original all or nothing offer. It would be unfair to interpret the long delay as a sign of prevarication, or an attempt on Cromwell's part to secure support for accepting the crown. On the contrary, by the time the Petition was formally presented to him on 31 March, Cromwell had already dismissed the crown as 'a feather in a man's hat', in a stormy meeting with senior army officers who were worried he might succumb to temptation. He first rejected the offer only three days later. It was only the persistence of Parliament, and Cromwell's characteristic desire to keep as many different opinions with him as he could (a trait that he seems to have rediscovered over this great issue), that strung the business out for so long. Cromwell really does seem to have been convinced that 'God has seemed providentially not only to strike at the family but at the name . . . I would not build Jericho again.'[8] It was not just the Stuarts, but kingship itself that had been divinely judged. Who was Cromwell to go against that? As before, he was prepared to seek God and deliberate for long enough to be persuaded that he was mistaken but, despite repeated attempts by some to change his mind, he stood firm.

What seems very clear is that Cromwell wasn't particularly troubled by potential opposition to his taking the crown. The nearest he came to flirting with acceptance was in his conversation with army officers who were opposed to it. On that occasion, he seems to have been so angered by the implication that he might want the title that he was prepared to set out its potential benefits. He acknowledged that some men might be tempted, but he wasn't. If Oliver Cromwell had wanted to be King Oliver, he could have been. The dynamics of this famous episode fall very much on the side of the crown pursuing Oliver, rather than Oliver pursuing the crown.

The title had been rejected, but Cromwell embraced many of the trappings of monarchy after the Humble Petition. His reinvestiture as Lord Protector on 27 June 1657, which was not required by the new constitution, was accordingly a far more ostentatious affair than the relatively self-effacing ceremony that had first settled the title on him. In the words of the hostile Lord Clarendon, it was 'nothing wanting to be a perfect formal coronation but a crown and an archbishop' – both of which, of course, had been abolished. But there was an oath, an ermine-lined robe with train, a presentation of the equivalent of the regalia – sword, sceptre and bible – as well as the nod to a coronation's role as moment of public acclamation. At the climax of the ceremony, in answer to the heralds' proclamation of Oliver, the audience shouted out, 'God save the Lord Protector'.

Much of what was important about the Protectorate had already happened before this apotheosis. The union with

Scotland and the substitution of Jamaica as the site of nascent imperial ambitions after the failure at Hispaniola had both preceded it. So too had the 'readmission' of the Jews, after the appeal of Rabbi Menasseh ben Israel of Amsterdam, in 1656. Of all the achievements of the Protectorate, this one can most squarely be attributed to Cromwell himself. The Council opposed it, but the Protector had met in person with the rabbi and was clearly persuaded by his arguments. Cromwell decided that as the Jewish expulsion in the Middle Ages had been a royal edict, he could personally authorize their readmission. His reasons are not entirely clear, and surely would have had little to do with modern notions of anti-discrimination. Cromwell had included the Jews among his list of the godly peoples who he hoped would live together, and he knew that Christ's reign on earth was to be preceded by their conversion. So it is possible that the new beginnings of British Judaism are owed to an urge to evangelism rather than toleration.

Oliver Cromwell died, aged fifty-nine, on 3 September 1658, the anniversary of his crushing victories at Dunbar and Worcester. He had been reinvested as Lord Protector less than fifteen months before. A king with such a short reign would have had little time to make much impression on history, and Cromwell's 'reign' was far from the most dramatic period in his life. Cromwell's eventual position at the head of the nation was a remarkable achievement, but the career that had brought him there is the reason he is remembered. The year before his final illness, a chest infection that developed into pneumonia that August, had seen a rise in the activities of those 'Commonwealthsmen' for whom Oliver's quasi-monarchy was too much to bear. In 1658, faced with the threat of an alliance between opposition republican elements in the army and in Parliament, he moved once again to dissolve the latter. Parliament had provided the means by which Cromwell first made a name for himself, but he had long since wearied of it. He was still confident, on the other hand, of his ability to bring the majority of the army with him. As well as dismissing the more troublesome officers, he knew how to appeal to the remainder, inviting 200 of them to a banquet in Whitehall two days after the dissolution, at which the guests declared in their cups their 'resolve to stand and fall, live and die, with my Lord Protector'.[9]

When he wasn't entertaining his former comrades and seeing off threats from republicans and Royalists alike, the Lord Protector continued to project a kingly persona, having his portrait painted on several occasions, and elevating his family with two aristocratic marriages for his daughters. Although Cromwell's court took up only around 3 per cent of government expenditure compared to Charles I's 40 per cent, it was a cultured and refined environment where choral music and 'mixed dancing' were encouraged, to the disappointment of some Puritan observers.[10] What survived of Charles's furniture, art and tapestries after the depredations of the Commonwealth were put on display in Cromwell's residences at Whitehall and Hampton Court. But if the Lord Protector managed to advertise an image of his Protectorate that gave it a wide legitimacy, allowing his regime to conduct high-level diplomacy with the

French, for example, he did not do enough to establish a succession. The Humble Petition empowered him to nominate his successor, but there is no certainty that he ever did. It is most likely that on his deathbed he nominated his eldest son Richard, but the fact that there is any doubt points up the contrast with a conventional royal succession. Even in a monarchy, the sovereign's nomination of a successor was no guarantee of a smooth transfer of power, but perhaps only Elizabeth I had resisted naming one for so long. To the last, Oliver delayed making the difficult decision, no doubt seeking the Lord before finally, as he lay dying, indicating that his son should follow him. Richard Cromwell thus came to the task woefully under-prepared. The Protectorate was never quite a personal cult, but the system behind Oliver was not strong enough to sustain a successor who was thrust into the job – even if he lasted longer than might have been predicted, until May the following year.

Oliver Cromwell was buried as a king. His effigy wore the 'cap of regality' – that is, as other observers put it, it had 'a crown on the head'. Though it was still as Lord Protector, rather than King Oliver, that he was laid to rest in Henry VIII's chapel in Westminster Abbey, in all other respects this ceremony, 'performed with very great majesty', was the royal recognition that Cromwell had gone to such lengths to avoid.[11] Its trappings still have the power to command attention today. In 2015, the inscribed copper gilt funeral plate later removed from the coffin was sold at auction for £70,000. Cromwell's body itself was, after the Restoration, subjected to much greater indignities: dug up, hanged and decapitated, with his severed head leading a colourful afterlife, during which it became something between a lucky charm and a historical exhibit. It would be hard to say whether Cromwell's own flirtation with kingship made the revenge or the curiosity any more intense.

Cromwell's legacy can be as difficult to locate as his physical remains. Much of it is negative, notable mainly for the reaction it provoked. After the Restoration, most of what Cromwell himself would have prized was overturned, including the relatively tolerant religious settlement that he had eventually overseen. The Protectorate's contributions to the 'sinews of power', the financial arrangements upon which the British Empire was based, are achievements too technical to have much popular traction. To a modern observer, wary again of the harm religious fanaticism can do on the political stage, Cromwell the zealot does not invite much empathy. But as well as the zeal that led him to the horrors of Drogheda and Wexford, he consistently displayed an urge to improve the religious lives (and to a lesser extent, and much less importantly to him, the lives *tout court*) not only of those with whom he was in sympathy, but also those with whom he disagreed. He was in many ways, to use his own word, 'unEnglish', both in his zeal and his tolerance. His resistance to the idea of monarchy was not unEnglish enough to lead him to a wholehearted support for republicanism, but the fact that it resulted in the unique experiment of the Protectorate is testimony to Cromwell's extraordinary power to bend events to his will. His most impassioned posthumous advocate, Thomas

Carlyle, compared him to Napoleon, because 'In rebellious ages, when Kingship itself seems dead and abolished, Cromwell, Napoleon step forth as kings.'[12] But, unlike the Emperor of the French, Cromwell demonstrated that it was possible to take a great nation's future in his hands without also taking a crown.

Notes

INTRODUCTION

1. 'A brief Relation of the late Dangerous Plot for the Destruction of his Highness's person', in John Towill Rutt (ed.), *Diary of Thomas Burton Esq*, vol. 2, April 1657–February 1658 (London: 1828), pp. 483–8 http://www.british-history. ac.uk/burton-diaries/vol2/pp483–488
2. *Mercurius Politicus*, no. 347 (29 January–4 February 1657), quoted in Patrick Little, 'John Thurloe and the Offer of the Crown to Oliver Cromwell', in Patrick Little (ed.), *Oliver Cromwell: New Perspectives* (Basingstoke: Palgrave Macmillan, 2009), p. 223.
3. Wilbur Cortez Abbott (ed.), *The Writings and Speeches of Oliver Cromwell* (Cambridge, Mass.: Harvard University Press, 1937–47), vol. 4, p. 412; and John Ashe MP in Little, 'John Thurloe and the Offer of the Crown to Oliver Cromwell', p. 221.

1. CHILDHOOD AND YOUTH

1. Abbott, *Writings and Speeches*, vol. 1, p. 97; Oliver St John was an eminent lawyer; Elizabeth was his second wife.
2. Simon Healy, '1636: The Unmaking of Oliver Cromwell?', in Little (ed.), *Oliver Cromwell: New Perspectives*, pp. 20–37.
3. Abbott, *Writings and Speeches*, vol. 1, p. 751 (quoting Joseph Spence, *Anecdotes, observations, and characters, of books and men: collected from the conversation of Mr Pope, and other eminent persons of his time*).
4. John Morrill, 'Cromwell, Oliver (1599–1658)', *Oxford Dictionary of National Biography* (Oxford: Oxford University Press, 2004).
5. Mark Kishlansky's chapter on the period in his Penguin Monarchs volume on Charles I (London: Allen Lane, 2014) is entitled 'Peace and Prosperity'.
6. *Calendar of State Papers Domestic: Charles I, 1631–3* (London: Her Majesty's Stationery Office, 1862), p. 501.

2. AT WESTMINSTER

1. TNA: PRO, SP 16/94/88 quoted in Anthony Milton, 'Laud, William (1573–1645)', *Oxford Dictionary of National Biography*; online edn, May 2009.

2. See Ian Gentles, *The English Revolution and the Wars in the Three Kingdoms 1638–1652* (Harlow: Pearson Longman, 2007), pp. 30–31.

3. Edward Hyde, Earl of Clarendon, ed. Paul Seaward, *The History of the Rebellion: A New Selection* (Oxford: Oxford University Press, 2009), p. 65.

4. Quoted in Stephen K. Roberts's essay, 'One That Would Sit Well at the Mark: The Early Parliamentary Career of Oliver Cromwell 1640–1642', in Little (ed.), *Oliver Cromwell*, p. 45.

5. Abbott, *Writings and Speeches*, vol. 1, p. 121, quoting Warwick's *Memoirs* (1701).

6. John Rushworth, 'Historical Collections: The impeachment of Edward Montagu', in *Historical Collections of Private Passages of State*, vol. 4, 1640–42 (London: 1721), pp. 473–94. British History Online http://www.british-history.ac.uk/rushworth-papers/vol4/pp473-494 [accessed 18 March 2016].

7. *Journal of the House of Commons*, vol. 2, 1640–43 (London: 1802), 5 January 1642, p. 369.

3. 'VALIANT COLONEL CROMWELL'

1. Abbott, *Writings and Speeches*, vol. 4, p. 471 (speech to Parliament, 13 April 1657).

2. Abbott, *Writings and Speeches*, vol. 1, p. 256.

3. Ibid., p. 299.

4. Description of Cromwell in *Kingdomes Weekly Intelligencer*, 25 July–1 August 1643, issue 28; 'Statement of an Opponent of Cromwell', in David Masson (ed.), *The Quarrel between the Earl of Manchester and Oliver Cromwell* (London: Camden Society, 1875), pp. 72–3.

5. Abbott, *Writings and Speeches*, vol. 1, pp. 266–7, quoting John Vicars, *God's Ark Overtopping the World's Waves* (1644).

6. *The Scotish Dove*, 13 October 1643–20 October 1643, issue 1.

7. Parliamentary statement to Scots commissioners, 23 October 1642 (Bodl. MS Tanner 64, fo.73), in Gentles, *The English Revolution and the Wars in the Three Kingdoms*, p. 76.

8. Solemn League and Covenant quoted in Gentles, ibid., pp. 208–9.

9. Hebrews 4:12; for Puritan reading habits see Andrew Cambers, *Godly Reading: Print, Manuscript and Puritanism in England, 1580–1720* (Cambridge: Cambridge University Press, 2011), pp. 2–3, 16–21.

10. Abbott, *Writings and Speeches*, vol. 1, pp. 278–9.

11. G. Trease, *Portrait of a Cavalier: William Cavendish, First Duke of Newcastle* (London: Macmillan, 1979), p. 141.

12. *Letters and Journals of Robert Baillie*, vol. 2 (Edinburgh: W. Gray, 1775), pp. 40–41.

13. Cromwell to Major-General Crawford, 10 March 1643, in Abbott, *Writings and Speeches*, vol. 1, p. 278.

14. Ibid., p. 299.

15. Ibid., p. 302.

16. John Bruce (ed.), *The Quarrel between the Earl of Manchester and Oliver Cromwell: An Episode of the English Civil War* (London: Camden Society, 1875), p. 75.

17. Abbott, *Writings and Speeches*, vol. 1, pp. 314–15.

18. Letter of Henry Moore Ward, 15 June 1645, printed in *The Weekly Account*, 18 June 1645.
19. Abbott, *Writings and Speeches*, vol. 1, p. 360.
20. Ibid., p. 377.

4. GENERAL AND REGICIDE

1. O. Ogle and W. H. Bliss (eds), *Calendar of the Clarendon State Papers Preserved in the Bodleian Library*, vol. 1, p. 361 (no. 2,439) (Oxford: Clarendon Press, 1872); the 'imposthume' phrase from the actual letter is quoted in C. H. Firth (ed.), *The Clarke Papers: Selections from the Papers of William Clarke, Secretary to the Council of the Army, 1647–1649, and to General Monck and the Commanders of the Army in Scotland, 1651–1660*, vol. 1, p. xviii (London: Camden Society, 1891). For psychosomatic diagnosis, see e.g. Antonia Fraser, *Cromwell: Our Chief of Men* (London: Weidenfeld & Nicolson, 1973), Chapter 6.
2. See Simon Healy, '1636: The Unmaking of Oliver Cromwell?', in Little (ed.), *Cromwell: New Perspectives*, p. 33.
3. See Peter Ackroyd, *Civil War: The History of England*, vol. 2 (London: Pan Books, 2015), p. 290, for an example of the continuing diagnosis of 'nervous strain' as a cause of Cromwell's condition.
4. Abbott, *Writings and Speeches*, vol. 1, p. 429.
5. Ibid., p. 439.
6. Ibid., pp. 449–50.
7. Firth (ed.), *Clarke Papers*, vol. 1, p. 73 and pp. 99–100, fn.
8. See J. C. Davis, 'Oliver Cromwell', in Michael J. Braddick (ed.), *The Oxford Handbook of the English Revolution* (Oxford: Oxford University Press, 2015), p. 230.
9. John Lilburne, *Jonah's Cry Out of the Whale's Belly* (1647), in Abbott, *Writings and Speeches*, vol. 1, p. 435.
10. Quoted in Austin Woolrych, *Britain in Revolution, 1625–1660* (Oxford: Oxford University Press, 2002), p. 361, where he reiterates an earlier reidentification of 'writer and addressee'.
11. John Rushworth, *Historical Collections of Private Passages of State*, vol. 6, 1645–7 (London: 1722), pp. 549–50.
12. 'Memoirs of Sir John Berkeley', in Francis Maseres (ed.), *Select Tracts Relating to the Civil Wars in England in the Reign of Charles I* (London: Wilks, 1815), vol. 1, p. 364.
13. Woolrych, *Britain in Revolution*, p. 374.
14. A. S. P. Woodhouse (ed.), *Puritanism and Liberty: Being the Army Debates (1647–9) from the Clarke Manuscripts with Supplementary Documents* (London: Dent, 1974), p. 53.
15. Abbott, *Writings and Speeches*, vol. 1, pp. 543–4.
16. Woolrych, *Britain in Revolution*, p. 408.
17. Abbott, *Writings and Speeches*, vol. 1, p. 638 and Rushworth, *Historical Collections*, vol. 7, 1647–8, pp. 1, 211.
18. *Memoirs of Edmund Ludlow*, in Abbott, *Writings and Speeches*, vol. 1, p. 708.
19. Ibid., p. 696.

20. Ibid., p. 737.
21. Ibid., p. 741.
22. Parliamentary Archives HL/PO/JO/10/297A. The one on display at the Royal Gallery is a facsimile.
23. Woolrych, *Britain in Revolution*, p. 437.
24. John Lilburne, *The Picture of the Councel of State* (1649), quoted in Peter Gaunt, *Oliver Cromwell* (Oxford: Blackwell, 1997), p. 110.
25. The Labour Party leader Jeremy Corbyn, asked to name the historical figure he most admired, chose Lilburne, a 'very interesting character, because of the way he managed to develop the whole debate about the English civil war into something very different' (*New Statesman*, 29 July 2015).
26. H. N. Brailsford, *The Levellers and the English Revolution* (Redwood, Calif.: Stanford University Press, 1961), p. 498.
27. Peter H. Wilson, *Europe's Tragedy: A New History of the Thirty Years War* (London: Allen Lane, 2009), p. 470.
28. Abbott, *Writings and Speeches*, vol. 2, pp. 124–7.
29. Edmund Ludlow and Lucy Hutchinson both thought that they had been taken in, on reflection. Abbott, *Writings and Speeches*, vol. 2, p. 268.
30. Letter to the General Assembly of the Kirk of Scotland, 3 August 1650, Abbott, *Writings and Speeches*, vol. 2, p. 303.
31. According to a witness recorded by John Aubrey, who also claimed that Cromwell had a laughing fit before Naseby. John Aubrey, *Miscellanies Upon Various Subjects* (London: W. Ottridge, 1784), pp. 160–61.
32. Letter to Speaker William Lenthall, 4 September 1650, Abbott, *Writings and Speeches*, vol. 2, p. 324.
33. Ibid., pp. 329, 404.
34. Bulstrode Whitelocke, *Memorials of the English Affairs* (London: 1682), pp. 491–2.
35. Kevin Sharpe, *Image Wars: Promoting Kings and Commonwealths in England, 1603–1660* (London and New Haven, Conn.: Yale University Press, 2010), p. 467.

5. LORD PROTECTOR

1. This pamphlet was published in 1649, but Cromwell had been singled out for ridicule as early as 1645, in John Cleveland's *The Character of a London Diurnall*. See discussion in Laura Lunger Knoppers, *Constructing Cromwell: Ceremony, Portrait and Print 1645–1661* (Cambridge: Cambridge University Press, 2009), pp. 10–30.
2. See Sharpe, *Image Wars*, pp. 494–5 for a discussion of this portrait, and Laura Lunger Knoppers, 'The Politics of Portraiture: Oliver Cromwell and the Plain Style', *Renaissance Quarterly* 51, no. 4 (1998), pp. 1282–1319. In 2014 the National Portrait Gallery placed its portraits of Heselrige and Cromwell side by side, with an (inconclusive) reproduction of the infra-red image of a painting beneath Heselrige's portrait.
3. Text of the Instrument of Government, 16 December 1653, in S. R. Gardiner (ed.), *The Constitutional Documents of the Puritan Revolution 1625–1660* (Oxford: Clarendon Press, 1899), p. 405.

4. The Lord Protector's Speech to the Parliament, 4 September 1654, in Abbott, *Writings and Speeches*, vol. 3, pp. 434–43.

5. Letter to Robert Hammond, in Abbott, *Writings and Speeches*, vol. 1, p. 677.

6. Abbott, *Writings and Speeches*, vol. 3, pp. 844–8.

7. Barry Coward, *The Cromwellian Protectorate* (Manchester: Manchester University Press, 2002), p. 79.

8. Abbott, *Writings and Speeches*, vol. 4, p. 460.

9. Sharpe, *Image Wars*, p. 518.

10. For expenditure, see G. E. Aylmer, *The King's Servants: The Civil Service of Charles I, 1625–1642* (London: Routledge & Kegan Paul, 1961), pp. 27, 436–7; the republican memoirist Lucy Hutchinson described a 'court full of sin and vanity': *Memoirs of the Life of Colonel Hutchinson* (London: H. G. Bohn, 1806), p. 370.

11. 'Cromwell's death and funeral order', in John Towill Rutt (ed.), *Diary of Thomas Burton Esq*, vol. 2, April 1657–February 1658 (London: 1828), pp. 516–30.

12. Thomas Carlyle, *On Heroes, Hero-Worship, and The Heroic in History* (London: James Fraser, 1841), VI, 'The Hero as King Cromwell, Napoleon: Modern Revolutionism', p. 329.

Further Reading

Cromwell's life has not been written about in full for a surprisingly long time. The last major biography for a general readership was Antonia Fraser's richly detailed, personal *Cromwell: Our Chief of Men* (London: Weidenfeld & Nicolson, 1973, most recently reissued 2008), which came not long after the more scholarly and politically focused but equally readable Life by Christopher Hill, *God's Englishman: Oliver Cromwell and the English Revolution* (London: Weidenfeld & Nicolson, 1970, and London: Penguin, 1990). Both these books remain the most rewarding biographical resources, though naturally some of their interpretations have been overtaken by more recent scholarship. Among shorter treatments, both Barry Coward, *Oliver Cromwell* (London: Longman, 1991) and Peter Gaunt, *Oliver Cromwell* (London: British Library Publishing, 2004) take modern scholarly approaches into account while telling the whole story energetically. Ian Gentles's *Oliver Cromwell: God's Warrior and the English Revolution* (Basingstoke: Palgrave Macmillan, 2010) opens up new lines of enquiry, including Cromwell's love life, as well as his soldiering, horse-breeding and lay preaching. John Morrill's lengthy entry on Cromwell in the *Oxford Dictionary of National Biography* (Oxford: Oxford University Press, 2004, online at http://www.oxforddnb.com, and subsequently published as a separate volume by the same press, 2007) is an ideal starting point for a clear, sympathetic but no-nonsense treatment.

Morrill is also one of the editors working on a promised five-volume Oxford University Press edition of 'all the writings and speeches of Oliver Cromwell', which will surely encourage a new generation of biographers (of whom one hopes Professor Morrill is one) to take on

Oliver in the round. Until then, the pioneering work of Thomas Carlyle, while still fascinating for a nineteenth-century view of seventeenth-century Puritanism (*The Letters and Speeches of Oliver Cromwell with elucidations*, London: Chapman and Hall, 1845) has given way to the four mighty volumes of Wilbur Cortez Abbott's *Writings and Speeches of Oliver Cromwell with an Introduction, Notes and a Sketch of His Life* (Cambridge, Mass.: Harvard University Press, 1937–47) and Ivan Roots's more reliable, if less compendious, *Speeches of Oliver Cromwell* (London: Dent, 1989).

Modern scholars, as well as hiving Oliver off into separate, manageable compartments (see John Morrill's edited essay collection *Oliver Cromwell and the English Revolution*, London: Longman, 1990), have increasingly realized that the huge quantity of Cromwell's own words can mislead as much as it can enlighten. Work informed by this spirit of thoughtful scepticism includes Patrick Little's edited collection *Oliver Cromwell: New Perspectives* (Basingstoke: Palgrave Macmillan, 2008) and J. C. Davis's volume in a series on Reputations (*Oliver Cromwell*, London: Bloomsbury Academic, 2001).

The Civil Wars that made Cromwell and unmade his opponent have continued to be the engine room of British historiography in the past two decades. This carries on a tradition that began just after the wars themselves, when the Royalist Earl of Clarendon, Edward Hyde, composed his *History of the Rebellion and Civil Wars in England* in six volumes (Oxford: Clarendon Press, 1888). There is a more manageable selection of Clarendon's history and memoirs available, edited by Paul Seaward: *The History of the Rebellion: A New Selection* (Oxford: Oxford University Press, 2009). Three of the best modern treatments of this unfailingly fascinating and confusing era are Austin Woolrych, *Britain in Revolution, 1625–1660* (Oxford: Oxford University Press, 2002), Michael Braddick, *God's Fury, England's Fire: A New History of the English Civil Wars* (London: Allen Lane, 2008) and Ian Gentles, *The English Revolution and the Wars of the Three Kingdoms, 1638–1652* (Harlow: Pearson Education, 2007), which is strongest on the military narrative. For a military view of

Oliver himself there is *Old Ironsides: The Military Biography of Oliver Cromwell* by Frank Kitson (London: Weidenfeld & Nicolson, 2004), while Ian Gentles's *The New Model Army in England, Ireland and Scotland, 1645–1653* (Oxford: Blackwell, 1992) is the definitive history of the fighting force that became a political actor in the drama.

Among the groups that rose to prominence through the army, the Levellers are the most intriguing. H. N. Brailsford's *The Levellers and the English Revolution* (Redwood, Calif.: Stanford University Press, 1961) is the classic study, supplemented now by Rachel Foxley's *The Levellers: Radical Political Thought in the English Revolution* (Manchester: Manchester University Press, 2013) and, too late to be of use in the writing of this book, John Rees's *The Leveller Revolution* (London: Verso, 2016). Christopher Hill edited Brailsford's posthumously published work, and his own publications on the Levellers and the other radical political and religious groups that sprang up during the Interregnum, particularly *The World Turned Upside Down: Radical Ideas during the English Revolution* (London: Penguin, 1975), brilliantly evoke and interrogate a unique English historical moment.

The period of the Protectorate has been variously portrayed as authoritarian, reactionary and dysfunctional. For a more even-handed treatment there is Barry Coward's *The Cromwellian Protectorate* (Manchester: Manchester University Press, 2002) and, for an overview of the whole period from the execution of Charles I to the Restoration, *The British Republic 1649–1660* by Ronald Hutton (Basingstoke: Macmillan, 2000). For Cromwell's attempt to fashion a new identity for his Protectorate, somewhere between regal and republican, and how that fitted into Stuart patterns, see Kevin Sharpe's *Image Wars: Promoting Kings and Commonwealths in England, 1603–1660* (London and New Haven, Conn.: Yale University Press, 2010). Finally, for the posthumous travels of Oliver's most famous body part, there is Jonathan Fitzgibbons's *Oliver's Head* (Kew: National Archives, 2008).

Picture Credits

1. Cromwell with crown, sceptre and orb (akg-images/British Library)
2a. One of the earliest known contemporary images of Cromwell, early 1640s (© National Portrait Gallery, London)
2b. John Lilburne, Leveller (Private Collection/Bridgeman Images)
3. Battle plan of Naseby on vellum (© British Library Board. All Rights Reserved/Bridgeman Images)
4a. Delaroche, Cromwell over Charles's body (akg-images)
4b. Hat of Judge Bradshaw (Ashmolean Museum, University of Oxford, UK/Bridgeman Images)
5. 'The World Turn'd Upside Down' (akg-images/British Library)
6a. Cromwell's reinvestiture as Lord Protector, 1657 (akg-images/British Library)
6b. Portrait of Cromwell as General by Robert Walker, 1649 (© National Portrait Gallery, London)
7a. Cromwell's letter to the House of Commons after the victory at Naseby, 1645 (The Stapleton Collection/Bridgeman Images)
7b. Cromwell's reply to a petition of the East India Company, 1657 (akg-images/World History Archive)
8a. Cromwell's death mask (© Mark Fiennes/Bridgeman Images)
8b. Copper gilt coffin plate (Sotheby's)

Acknowledgements

It came as something of a surprise that a shortish book demands almost as much work as a longer one, and is just as much of a team effort. Thomas Penn at Penguin has been a scrupulously attentive and positive editor. Tom, Anna Hervé, Linden Lawson and Chloe Currens have made it a pleasure to write this book. My agent, Peter Straus, brought the Penguin Monarchs series to my attention before the books had started to come out, and encouraged me to take on the Cromwellian exception. Professor Ronald Hutton of Bristol University, who includes Cromwell and the Civil Wars among his many areas of expertise, was kind enough to read my text, and save me from the worst of my misapprehensions. At my work, two editors, Peter Stothard and Stig Abell, have cheerfully allowed me time to moonlight. At home, as always, Jules has unfailingly made space in a busier life to give me time to write, while my sons, Jude and Johan, have put up with another intruder from the distant past. As Oliver would have put it, 'I am in good earnest thankful'.

Index

Penguin Monarchs

THE HOUSES OF WESSEX AND DENMARK

Athelstan*	Tom Holland
Aethelred the Unready	Richard Abels
Cnut	Ryan Lavelle
Edward the Confessor	

THE HOUSES OF NORMANDY, BLOIS AND ANJOU

William I*	Marc Morris
William II	John Gillingham
Henry I	Edmund King
Stephen	Carl Watkins
Henry II*	Richard Barber
Richard I	Thomas Asbridge
John	Nicholas Vincent

THE HOUSE OF PLANTAGENET

Henry III	Stephen Church
Edward I*	Andy King
Edward II	Christopher Given-Wilson
Edward III*	Jonathan Sumption
Richard II*	Laura Ashe

THE HOUSES OF LANCASTER AND YORK

Henry IV	Catherine Nall
Henry V*	Anne Curry
Henry VI	James Ross
Edward IV	A. J. Pollard
Edward V	Thomas Penn
Richard III	Rosemary Horrox

* Now in paperback

THE HOUSE OF TUDOR

Henry VII	Sean Cunningham
Henry VIII*	John Guy
Edward VI*	Stephen Alford
Mary I*	John Edwards
Elizabeth I	Helen Castor

THE HOUSE OF STUART

James I	Thomas Cogswell
Charles I*	Mark Kishlansky
[Cromwell*	David Horspool]
Charles II*	Clare Jackson
James II	David Womersley
William III & Mary II*	Jonathan Keates
Anne	Richard Hewlings

THE HOUSE OF HANOVER

George I	Tim Blanning
George II	Norman Davies
George III	Amanda Foreman
George IV	Stella Tillyard
William IV	Roger Knight
Victoria*	Jane Ridley

THE HOUSES OF SAXE-COBURG & GOTHA AND WINDSOR

Edward VII*	Richard Davenport-Hines
George V*	David Cannadine
Edward VIII*	Piers Brendon
George VI*	Philip Ziegler
Elizabeth II*	Douglas Hurd

* Now in paperback

ALLEN LANE
an imprint of
PENGUIN BOOKS

Also Published

Stephen Kotkin, *Stalin, Vol. II: Waiting for Hitler, 1928-1941*

Lindsey Fitzharris, *The Butchering Art: Joseph Lister's Quest to Transform the Grisly World of Victorian Medicine*

Serhii Plokhy, *Lost Kingdom: A History of Russian Nationalism from Ivan the Great to Vladimir Putin*

Mark Mazower, *What You Did Not Tell: A Russian Past and the Journey Home*

Lawrence Freedman, *The Future of War: A History*

Niall Ferguson, *The Square and the Tower: Networks, Hierarchies and the Struggle for Global Power*

Matthew Walker, *Why We Sleep: The New Science of Sleep and Dreams*

Edward O. Wilson, *The Origins of Creativity*

John Bradshaw, *The Animals Among Us: The New Science of Anthropology*

David Cannadine, *Victorious Century: The United Kingdom, 1800-1906*

Leonard Susskind and Art Friedman, *Special Relativity and Classical Field Theory*

Maria Alyokhina, *Riot Days*

Oona A. Hathaway and Scott J. Shapiro, *The Internationalists: And Their Plan to Outlaw War*

Chris Renwick, *Bread for All: The Origins of the Welfare State*

Anne Applebaum, *Red Famine: Stalin's War on Ukraine*

Richard McGregor, *Asia's Reckoning: The Struggle for Global Dominance*

Chris Kraus, *After Kathy Acker: A Biography*

Clair Wills, *Lovers and Strangers: An Immigrant History of Post-War Britain*

Odd Arne Westad, *The Cold War: A World History*

Max Tegmark, *Life 3.0: Being Human in the Age of Artificial Intelligence*

Jonathan Losos, *Improbable Destinies: How Predictable is Evolution?*

Chris D. Thomas, *Inheritors of the Earth: How Nature Is Thriving in an Age of Extinction*

Chris Patten, *First Confession: A Sort of Memoir*

James Delbourgo, *Collecting the World: The Life and Curiosity of Hans Sloane*

Naomi Klein, *No Is Not Enough: Defeating the New Shock Politics*

Ulrich Raulff, *Farewell to the Horse: The Final Century of Our Relationship*

Slavoj Žižek, *The Courage of Hopelessness: Chronicles of a Year of Acting Dangerously*

Patricia Lockwood, *Priestdaddy: A Memoir*

Ian Johnson, *The Souls of China: The Return of Religion After Mao*

Stephen Alford, *London's Triumph: Merchant Adventurers and the Tudor City*

Hugo Mercier and Dan Sperber, *The Enigma of Reason: A New Theory of Human Understanding*

Stuart Hall, *Familiar Stranger: A Life Between Two Islands*

Allen Ginsberg, *The Best Minds of My Generation: A Literary History of the Beats*

Sayeeda Warsi, *The Enemy Within: A Tale of Muslim Britain*

Alexander Betts and Paul Collier, *Refuge: Transforming a Broken Refugee System*

Robert Bickers, *Out of China: How the Chinese Ended the Era of Western Domination*

Erica Benner, *Be Like the Fox: Machiavelli's Lifelong Quest for Freedom*

William D. Cohan, *Why Wall Street Matters*

David Horspool, *Oliver Cromwell: The Protector*

Daniel C. Dennett, *From Bacteria to Bach and Back: The Evolution of Minds*

Derek Thompson, *Hit Makers: How Things Become Popular*

Harriet Harman, *A Woman's Work*

Wendell Berry, *The World-Ending Fire: The Essential Wendell Berry*

Daniel Levin, *Nothing but a Circus: Misadventures among the Powerful*

Stephen Church, *Henry III: A Simple and God-Fearing King*

Pankaj Mishra, *Age of Anger: A History of the Present*

Graeme Wood, *The Way of the Strangers: Encounters with the Islamic State*

Michael Lewis, *The Undoing Project: A Friendship that Changed the World*

John Romer, *A History of Ancient Egypt, Volume 2: From the Great Pyramid to the Fall of the Middle Kingdom*

Andy King, *Edward I: A New King Arthur?*

Thomas L. Friedman, *Thank You for Being Late: An Optimist's Guide to Thriving in the Age of Accelerations*

John Edwards, *Mary I: The Daughter of Time*

Grayson Perry, *The Descent of Man*

Deyan Sudjic, *The Language of Cities*

Norman Ohler, *Blitzed: Drugs in Nazi Germany*

Carlo Rovelli, *Reality Is Not What It Seems: The Journey to Quantum Gravity*

Catherine Merridale, *Lenin on the Train*

Susan Greenfield, *A Day in the Life of the Brain: The Neuroscience of Consciousness from Dawn Till Dusk*

Christopher Given-Wilson, *Edward II: The Terrors of Kingship*

Emma Jane Kirby, *The Optician of Lampedusa*

Minoo Dinshaw, *Outlandish Knight: The Byzantine Life of Steven Runciman*

Candice Millard, *Hero of the Empire: The Making of Winston Churchill*

Christopher de Hamel, *Meetings with Remarkable Manuscripts*

Brian Cox and Jeff Forshaw, *Universal: A Guide to the Cosmos*

Ryan Avent, *The Wealth of Humans: Work and Its Absence in the Twenty-first Century*

Jodie Archer and Matthew L. Jockers, *The Bestseller Code*

Cathy O'Neil, *Weapons of Math Destruction: How Big Data Increases Inequality and Threatens Democracy*

Peter Wadhams, *A Farewell to Ice: A Report from the Arctic*

Richard J. Evans, *The Pursuit of Power: Europe, 1815-1914*

Anthony Gottlieb, *The Dream of Enlightenment: The Rise of Modern Philosophy*

Marc Morris, *William I: England's Conqueror*

Gareth Stedman Jones, *Karl Marx: Greatness and Illusion*

J.C.H. King, *Blood and Land: The Story of Native North America*

Robert Gerwarth, *The Vanquished: Why the First World War Failed to End, 1917-1923*

Joseph Stiglitz, *The Euro: And Its Threat to Europe*

John Bradshaw and Sarah Ellis, *The Trainable Cat: How to Make Life Happier for You and Your Cat*

A J Pollard, *Edward IV: The Summer King*

Erri de Luca, *The Day Before Happiness*

Diarmaid MacCulloch, *All Things Made New: Writings on the Reformation*

Daniel Beer, *The House of the Dead: Siberian Exile Under the Tsars*

Tom Holland, *Athelstan: The Making of England*

Christopher Goscha, *The Penguin History of Modern Vietnam*

Mark Singer, *Trump and Me*

Roger Scruton, *The Ring of Truth: The Wisdom of Wagner's Ring of the Nibelung*

Ruchir Sharma, *The Rise and Fall of Nations: Ten Rules of Change in the Post-Crisis World*

Jonathan Sumption, *Edward III: A Heroic Failure*

Daniel Todman, *Britain's War: Into Battle, 1937-1941*

Dacher Keltner, *The Power Paradox: How We Gain and Lose Influence*

Tom Gash, *Criminal: The Truth About Why People Do Bad Things*

Brendan Simms, *Britain's Europe: A Thousand Years of Conflict and Cooperation*

Slavoj Žižek, *Against the Double Blackmail: Refugees, Terror, and Other Troubles with the Neighbours*

Lynsey Hanley, *Respectable: The Experience of Class*

Piers Brendon, *Edward VIII: The Uncrowned King*

Matthew Desmond, *Evicted: Poverty and Profit in the American City*

T.M. Devine, *Independence or Union: Scotland's Past and Scotland's Present*

Seamus Murphy, *The Republic*

Jerry Brotton, *This Orient Isle: Elizabethan England and the Islamic World*

Srinath Raghavan, *India's War: The Making of Modern South Asia, 1939-1945*

Clare Jackson, *Charles II: The Star King*

Nandan Nilekani and Viral Shah, *Rebooting India: Realizing a Billion Aspirations*

Sunil Khilnani, *Incarnations: India in 50 Lives*

Helen Pearson, *The Life Project: The Extraordinary Story of Our Ordinary Lives*

Ben Ratliff, *Every Song Ever: Twenty Ways to Listen to Music Now*

Richard Davenport-Hines, *Edward VII: The Cosmopolitan King*

Peter H. Wilson, *The Holy Roman Empire: A Thousand Years of Europe's History*

Todd Rose, *The End of Average: How to Succeed in a World that Values Sameness*

Frank Trentmann, *Empire of Things: How We Became a World of Consumers, from the Fifteenth Century to the Twenty-First*

Laura Ashe, *Richard II: A Brittle Glory*

John Donvan and Caren Zucker, *In a Different Key: The Story of Autism*

Jack Shenker, *The Egyptians: A Radical Story*

Tim Judah, *In Wartime: Stories from Ukraine*

Serhii Plokhy, *The Gates of Europe: A History of Ukraine*

Robin Lane Fox, *Augustine: Conversions and Confessions*

Peter Hennessy and James Jinks, *The Silent Deep: The Royal Navy Submarine Service Since 1945*

Sean McMeekin, *The Ottoman Endgame: War, Revolution and the Making of the Modern Middle East, 1908–1923*

Charles Moore, *Margaret Thatcher: The Authorized Biography, Volume Two: Everything She Wants*

Dominic Sandbrook, *The Great British Dream Factory: The Strange History of Our National Imagination*

Larissa MacFarquhar, *Strangers Drowning: Voyages to the Brink of Moral Extremity*

Niall Ferguson, *Kissinger: 1923-1968: The Idealist*

Carlo Rovelli, *Seven Brief Lessons on Physics*

Tim Blanning, *Frederick the Great: King of Prussia*

Ian Kershaw, *To Hell and Back: Europe, 1914–1949*

Pedro Domingos, *The Master Algorithm: How the Quest for the Ultimate Learning Machine Will Remake Our World*

David Wootton, *The Invention of Science: A New History of the Scientific Revolution*

Christopher Tyerman, *How to Plan a Crusade: Reason and Religious War in the Middle Ages*

Andy Beckett, *Promised You A Miracle: UK 80–82*

Carl Watkins, *Stephen: The Reign of Anarchy*

Anne Curry, *Henry V: From Playboy Prince to Warrior King*

John Gillingham, *William II: The Red King*

Roger Knight, *William IV: A King at Sea*

Douglas Hurd, *Elizabeth II: The Steadfast*

Richard Nisbett, *Mindware: Tools for Smart Thinking*

Jochen Bleicken, *Augustus: The Biography*

Paul Mason, *PostCapitalism: A Guide to Our Future*

Frank Wilczek, *A Beautiful Question: Finding Nature's Deep Design*

Roberto Saviano, *Zero Zero Zero*

Owen Hatherley, *Landscapes of Communism: A History Through Buildings*

César Hidalgo, *Why Information Grows: The Evolution of Order, from Atoms to Economies*

Aziz Ansari and Eric Klinenberg, *Modern Romance: An Investigation*

Sudhir Hazareesingh, *How the French Think: An Affectionate Portrait of an Intellectual People*

Steven D. Levitt and Stephen J. Dubner, *When to Rob a Bank: A Rogue Economist's Guide to the World*

Leonard Mlodinow, *The Upright Thinkers: The Human Journey from Living in Trees to Understanding the Cosmos*

Hans Ulrich Obrist, *Lives of the Artists, Lives of the Architects*

Richard H. Thaler, *Misbehaving: The Making of Behavioural Economics*

Sheldon Solomon, Jeff Greenberg and Tom Pyszczynski, *Worm at the Core: On the Role of Death in Life*

Nathaniel Popper, *Digital Gold: The Untold Story of Bitcoin*

Dominic Lieven, *Towards the Flame: Empire, War and the End of Tsarist Russia*

Noel Malcolm, *Agents of Empire: Knights, Corsairs, Jesuits and Spies in the Sixteenth-Century Mediterranean World*

James Rebanks, *The Shepherd's Life: A Tale of the Lake District*

David Brooks, *The Road to Character*

Joseph Stiglitz, *The Great Divide*

Ken Robinson and Lou Aronica, *Creative Schools: Revolutionizing Education from the Ground Up*

Clotaire Rapaille and Andrés Roemer, *Move UP: Why Some Cultures Advances While Others Don't*

Jonathan Keates, *William III and Mary II: Partners in Revolution*

David Womersley, *James II: The Last Catholic King*

Richard Barber, *Henry II: A Prince Among Princes*

Jane Ridley, *Victoria: Queen, Matriarch, Empress*

John Gray, *The Soul of the Marionette: A Short Enquiry into Human Freedom*

Emily Wilson, *Seneca: A Life*